THE PROTOCOL FOR CORRECTION
OF BIRTH TIME

Ciro Discepolo

THE PROTOCOL FOR CORRECTION OF BIRTH TIME

A Practical Method to Correct Your Birth Time

Ricerca '90 Publisher

Translation and editing: Luciano Drusetta and Ram Ramakrishnan
Graphic design: Pino Valente

Copyright © 2011 Edizioni Ricerca '90

Viale Gramsci, 16
80122 Napoli - ITALY
info@cirodiscepolo.it

www.solarreturns.com
www.cirodiscepolo.it

ISBN 978-88-964-4708-6
Printed in USA

Birth time rectification is the fundamental starting point to any serious study in Astrology
Ciro Discepolo

The birth data of the people mentioned in this book proceed mainly from Lois M. Rodden's database and from Ciro Discepolo's archives. Other birth data are taken from web-based databases.

Astral maps and calculations are produced by the exceptionally precise astrological software **Astral** and **Aladino** (also referred to as *Module for the Automatized Research of the Aimed Solar Returns 'RSMA'*).

Preface

The way we conduct an interrogation with a student who wishes to discover the exact hour of his birth is very important in my protocol of correction of hour of birth.

Let us use an example. In homeopathic medicine too, the interrogation of the patient is very important. The doctor asks his patient: "Are you sensitive to cold or to heat?"

"Yes, I am sensitive to cold."

"Let us verify this. Do you wear polo-neck sweaters or unbuttoned shirts in the winter?"

"The latter."

"Do you work with your chair near the heater or having the window open?"

"The second."

"When you go to sleep, do you crave for warmth or coldness for your feet, under the sheets?"

"The second."

"Very well, my friend, you are not sensitive to cold, but exactly the opposite."

As you can observe reading this bit of an interrogation, it is possible to arrive at a completely wrong result and it needs all the ability of the questioner to discover the long list of naïve lies that could be misleading in every kind of questioning process.

I will try to extend this concept to a longer interrogation that I once subjected my wife to, whom I had just met, to discover her true hour of birth that I thought was about 02:35 pm.

"Daniela, please, pay great attention to whatever that you do today and tomorrow, because from the ephemeris, I see that it is during this period that Mars will enter your natal Third House. It means that, if I am right, you will have some troubles, one or more 'bee-stings' in relation to the meanings of the Third House: cars, motorcycles, bicycles, transports, the road crossing, communications and telecommunications troubles, problems with couriers, phones, Internet, etc."

The evening of the following day, I asked her, "Daniela, have you had any of those bee-stings?"

"No, I did not experience anything of this kind."

"Well, please, sit down and talk to me for a while."

"Let start from yesterday morning. Did anything happen when you left your house and took your car?"

"No, noth… Just a moment: I remember. I met two policemen who fined me for parking in a wrong manner."

"Well, we have the first bee-sting. After this incident, did you move without other problems?"

"Actually, I had another little problem: my key did not work for some minutes and it happened several times yesterday and today."

"Ok, did you get to your office without other problems?"

"Just a little: yesterday, and even today, I felt a little uncomfortable because I feared a car crash."

"Then, at this moment, we can say that you had many bee-stings from yesterday morning until now: is it right?"

"Yes, it is."

"OK, let me continue. When, you arrived in your office yesterday, did the morning pass without troubles?"

"Yes, everything went well!"

"And what did you work at?"

"Oh, I was very busy unpacking my winter collection that had just arrived."

"Then you are telling me that yesterday the courier arrived?"

"Yes."

"And was the delivery OK?"

"NOOO! Nothing was OK: I had ordered two small pink shirts and instead they shipped two large pink shirts and so it was for all the other items of the expedition!!!"

"Then, my dear Daniela, as you see, you had a lot of bee-stings from yesterday to now and we can say that surely Mars entered your Third House between yesterday and today and the birth hour of 02:35 pm is confirmed once again…"

Dear Readers, this example is to offer you an operative mode to proceed with my protocol of correction of birth hour. If you will follow this method of interrogation, I can assure you that you will be able to discover the exact birth hour for everyone, but don't forget that one swallow doesn't make a summer. We have to repeat this exercise for three years, consecutively and collecting all congruous results, meaning that I will not have a month in which Mars enters 5 days earlier than expected and two months later Mars enters 5 days later then expected: WE HAVE TO OBTAIN THAT EVERY TIME MARS ENTERS EXACTLY ON THE EXPECTED DAY!

Good work!

Ciro Discepolo

Napoli, November 11th 2010

1.
The rectification of the time of birth

This is the first real big problem to solve, if you want to work properly on a natal chart. It is quite a complex exercise. Many believe they can solve it quickly and easily, while it is a multifaceted job in reality, a task that can be solved satisfactorily only after years of studies. Many great authors in the history of astrology have tried their hand at it. At the beginning of my study of astrology, I used to absorb, a bit uncritically, everything said by everyone. Later, I tested several of those methods of rectification, but they all soon proved to be totally inefficient.

Let us do this exercise in an orderly fashion. First of all let me explain why the times of birth (I am referring especially to those born during or before the sixties of the last century) are almost always (maybe in 99% of the cases?) rounded up. Let us consider how the process of delivery takes place, or how it used to take place. The baby is born and nobody among those present is actually standing there with a stopwatch in his hand to mark the exact time of the first cry.

Everyone thinks immediately to care for the baby, to wash it, clean it, preparing it to bring it to the mother or the nursery. Only at the end of these operations, someone looks at the clock and writes down this time on the bracelet that is applied to the baby's wrist – while it actually was born ten to twenty (some times, even thirty) minutes earlier. It goes without saying that it is possible that the opposite could happen: that the time of birth is rounded down. I think this is a first important and basic rule that we should adhere to – that of being wary of the reported time of birth particularly for births that occurred either around noon or midnight.

Let me elaborate. In the first case the mythologies related with the symbolic value of noon are so many and so important that they exert a tremendous psychological force in the minds of parents, relatives and those dealing with the delivery. For a mother, being able to claim, "My son was born on the twelfth stroke of noon" is such a persuasive charm that even if the baby was actually born at 12:40, in her mind she really 'forces' it to be born at 12 *o'clock*! In this regard, if one day I wanted to list all these and other myths so to compile a whole dossier on the lies (most of them told in good faith) that I have been told on the timing of birth, I could write a text far more voluminous than this book. For example, I remember a mother in her fifties, still shiny with the mind, who accompanied her daughter at the counselling. She said, "Look, do not waste your time with her time of birth! I remember as if it were today: it was Sunday and the twelfth stroke of noon could be heard..." As she spoke I checked on my computer and gave her the bad news: *that* day was not Sunday – it was Tuesday in fact.

The majority of parents (and as a consequence, the counselees themselves) are ready to swear on the Baby Jesus, on the Holy Mary, and on all the Saints, that they can not be wrong because at the time of delivery there was a huge clock on the wall, therefore... Fantasies, myths, dreams... If you accept them uncritically, you are lost: all your studies go to the dogs... Precisely about noon, when in ancient times I used to collaborate with the monthly Italian magazine of astrology *ASTRA* writing portraits of celebrities under Giuseppe Botteri's editorship, I happened to imagine that something similar might have happened with the recorded time of birth of Piero Chiara, a writer whom I really loved. After a few weeks of his portrait being published, he sent me a long letter in which he congratulated me and above all, he wrote that he had especially noted the correctness of my observations on his time of birth, which had been the victim, like many others, of the *mythology of noon*.

Not to mention midnight: the most unlikely things may happen if the time of birth is supposed to be at midnight. Not too long ago there were severe penalties if the child was not declared within a certain number of days from birth, and the latecomers had no other choice but to declare a time of birth delayed by several hours (sometimes days). When someone comes to me admitting that he can not even be sure of the day he was born, I immediately refuse to deal with him as an astrologer.

Still, in connection with the times of birth running around midnight, there are a number of reasons mostly of superstitious or – conversely – well-meaning kind that can spur people to declare a fictional time of birth to the authorities. For example, say that the child was delivered at 1:30 am, and also suppose that the previous day coincided with the name day of one of its grandparents. This may trigger a simulation of the real day of birth – in the past years even the nurses in the delivery room were willing to be party to it. Conversely, the time of birth can be modified by many hours by those parents who do not want their child to be born on the 17th of a month or in any other day commonly considered inauspicious. Sometimes, as years go by, the parents themselves forget that they had 'fixed' the time of birth. But as an astrologer, you may be able to expose this piece of false information through a long session of questioning of your counselee. In this case, your questions shall necessarily refer to the names of the patron Saints of the town where your counselee was born, the names of all his relatives, as well as the most relevant dates of events associated with the family and so on.

Typically everyone agrees that the times of birth are usually wrong, but everybody is convinced that *his or her own* time is correct to the minute! And as I mentioned, they call into question Saints, Madonnas and other gods...

Do not let them impress you with anything – simply go your way. In this case, suspicion should guide you like Virgil guided Dante: beware of anything and of everything, even of your own primary beliefs. Proceed trying to undermine even your own assumptions. Only in this way you have the opportunity to do a useful service to your counselees.

When I go around Italy to hold lectures, it often happens that people from the audience ask me something about their own astral chart. They may claim to be born, say, at 5:57 or 5:58 pm. Sometimes, it's people of forty years or more. So I ask them, "Has this time been rectified by you or by an astrologer?" The answer is frequently affirmative with regard to the first option, so I exhort, "Dare to do more, do not stop at an amendment of two or three minutes because, usually, the actual error is fifteen to thirty minutes – or even many more."

I mentioned earlier that at the beginning of my study of astrology, I used to follow many methods to rectify the time of birth; each advocated by some practioner of the science and elaborated in their writings. What aroused in me a charm, for its vaunted potential for *absolute* verification, was the method of primary directions set out by Reinhold Ebertin in his books. Reinhold Ebertin – along with André Barbault, Henri J. Gouchon and Angelo Brunini – has been and still is one of my absolute points of reference as an astrologer. He claimed that with the primary directions it is possible to forecast even the very day of an important event in one's life. His method was quite simple and straightforward. He claimed that starting from your estimated time of birth you should proceed by going back and forth by the minute, until you reach a time in relation to which you will be able to find, with the precision of the day, a decisive event in your life, such as – for example – marriage. When you have found it, that's it: *that* is your true time of birth! Galvanized by such an emphatic promise, I rushed myself headlong into that research, in which I would spend three to four years of deep studies in my life as an astrologer. What I said to myself was, "If I work with primary directions with the aim of obtaining the utmost accuracy, then I had rather proceed with the *only true primary directions*, i.e. those explained by Mr. Gouchon – who certainly is the greatest expert in this field." According to Gouchon, primary directions should take into account the latitude (both terrestrial and celestial latitude) in a birth chart.

It was a huge undertaking: simply adding the latitudinal position to the computation implied a logarithmic intricacy in calculations that were already quite complex in their original version. There were a few American programs of astrology that circulated in those years claiming to be able to calculate the true primary directions, but they actually calculated inaccurate ones.

So I decided to assemble the piece of software by myself with the help of some computer geeks, who were above all expert in mathematics and spherical trigonometry. I myself had to dust off my high school knowledge of trigonometry. The whole process took me, as I said, over three years only to develop the program. To calibrate it I made use of an astrologer colleague who, in my opinion – at least in those days – was the only one able to calculate the true primary directions: Claude Weiss in Zurich. Many print-outs, as well as many Swiss francs, travelled between my hometown and the larger city of Switzerland. At the end I delivered my program at its 99%. What I mean is that it coincided perfectly with the calculations of my Swiss colleague, but in one case out of a hundred it mistook one direction in such a blatant manner that everybody could notice the error at first sight.

"At this point – I thought – I've done it. What is left is to have the computer produce *a large number of* printouts." Thus I would get one hundred years of primary directions of my life; each print-out would be calculated on a different time of birth; each time of birth would be different (of one minute more or one minute less) from all the others. When I found the print-out that indicated the exact day of my wedding in the midst of mountains of paper, I would judge that my task had come to an end. The sad surprise was that on that same print-out (calculated for my alleged *real* birth time) all the other important events of my life (the births of my daughters, deaths of relatives, major works, etc.) were mistaken by several months, if not several years. However this experience, like all experiences, was not useless. On the contrary, it was an important part of my training. In fact, I was able to implant in myself an attitude towards astrology (and towards research in general), which is perhaps the best value that I can boast of: I am referring to my earnest opposition to any sort of fundamentalism of thought.

For example I distrust a lot of those who tell me that one of the variables that I have found can not be true because Ptolemy didn't write about it or because it would jeopardize the existence of the alleged twelfth planet X. Personally I begin to believe that (in astrology as elsewhere) something has the force of law only after I've tested it thousands of times – and even then I am not at all convinced that I should carve it down on the tables of the Bible. The only exception to this is the variable of astral heredity, which Luigi Miele and I have been able to demonstrate to be highly significant in statistical terms.

But let us stick to the rectification of the time of birth. Many years ago a lady came to me who was very passionate about astrology. She was born during the World War II under an air raid. The town hall of her place of birth was destroyed in that bombing and both her parents died when she was very young. No relatives had direct or indirect news of her birth: total darkness on those twenty-four hours. She asked if I could help rebuild her time of birth. I replied that I was not interested in that, professionally speaking: I should have worked for several months exclusively on her case.

No compensation would have been enough for such work, unless… I suggested I would use her case to write an essay. So it happened: I studied her case and several months later my book *La ricerca dell'ora di nascita* (*The search for the time of birth*) would be brought out by Blue Diamond Publisher. This booklet was sold out many years ago and never republished since. In return I asked her to work for at least one month on her detailed biography: she was supposed to tell me virtually everything about herself. So she did. *I* also worked for several weeks filling dozens of charts studying, in particular, the main transits and Solar Returns of her life. Eventually I felt that I had achieved a quite satisfactory result, but I also admitted that such a method was impractical because it is too expensive in terms of time.

Over the years I have developed another method, the one that I explain in this volume. I think it is quite valid, though not an 'absolute' one. For I believe that there is nothing absolute in this world.

My present approach involves three different phases. It is only applicable when you can start with an uncertainty of no more that about one–one and a half hour from the alleged (or officially recorded) time of birth. If it's only possible, ask the counselee to produce an original full birth certificate. Also ask him or her to produce a parental statement concerning the time of birth. After that, if based on these two statements the uncertainty on the time of birth can be reduced to a maximum of 90 minutes, proceed as follows:

1) Conducting an interview.

This is a very important stage. It can not be made by telephone; you must have the physical presence of your counselee. After asking the most appropriate questions, in the overwhelming majority of cases I am able to decide whether it is possible to proceed with studying the native's astral situation or if it's better not to deal with him or her as an astrologer.

2) Placing some 'sensors' in the native's next three or four Aimed Solar Returns.

For example, say that I relocate the counselee's SR to a place where Jupiter is at the MC. Now, if I can also place Mars of SR in the Third House of the relocated Solar Return, four to five degrees from the cusp of the Fourth House, this would be of enormous help to me. In fact one year later, when the counselee reports the main event of the past months covered by that SR, depending on Mars being in the 3rd or in the 4th House I would be able to understand much more about the native's real time of birth.

3) For at least three years, the counselee should study the ingress of Mars in the Houses of his/her own natal chart.

I will soon explain in detail these three steps. I believe that if they are applied according to the rules detailed in this book, they will allow everyone to approach very close to the real time of birth of their counselees.

If this may be of interest, I personally can say that after several years of study, this method helped me ascertain that I was actually born at 5:40 am (while according to both my birth record and my father's memory, I was born at 6 o'clock). This rectified time of birth is consistent to the degree and to the day with the 'sensors' of my ASR's, as well as with the entrances of Mars in my natal Houses.

2.
The Sun in the twelve natal Houses

Sun in the First House

I have no difficulty in admitting that it is not easy to describe typical features of the position of the Sun in the First House in a person who sits in front of me. Consider that the astrology that I deal with does not start from 'absolute theorems'.

It is not based on constraints such as 'traps and snares', i.e. prejudicial rules claiming that (just to give one example) if a truth has not been discovered by Ptolemy himself, it can not be true. *My* astrology is based on a great respect for Tradition, although corrected by the most modern studies – in particular those of the astrologer who, in my view, has been able to coagulate thousands of drops of the most precious ancient and modern knowledge (I am referring to André Barbault). Thus *my* astrology believes only in what a long practical career has been teaching me for almost thirty-five years of intense, passionate and uninterrupted study, to which I often devoted many sleepless nights. Thus I am free from all preconceived forms of puzzle boxes in which, for an alleged plot plan, everything must match the card which is beside, and all the tiles must create a comprehensive and precise mosaic.

As free as I am from all that, I can accept the idea that man is still unable to explain many things. Taking good note of this, I record into a sort of temporary file those results of my practical research that appear to have overwhelming evidence.

So in this case instead of pretending to reel off the… multiplication tables that we had to learn by rote, I prefer admitting that I haven't found any distinctive common feature in natives born with the Sun in their natal First House – and there are thousands of such people in my files…

During the interview, if I happen to talk with a native whose natal Sun could be in the First House, rather than looking for a confirmation of this hypothesis I investigate trying to exclude that the Sun may possibly lie in the Twelfth or in the Second House – both positions whose features are described below.

Of course – although it seems unnecessary to recount it – I rely on the canonical analysis of those dictates (of Tradition or not) that should mark unambiguously the position of the Sun in a determined House.

For example, among the many variables, a Sun in the First House should correspond to a very strong personality, an individual who usually takes quick and sharp decisions – in other words: a Ram-like behaviour. In this I might certainly recognize the prevailing feature of my own character; but I have also known dozens of individuals who – on the contrary – with the Sun in their natal First House behave like a 'sheep' with uncertain, weak personality. You know that any of the twelve solar signs may be of a 'compensated' type: yet in my opinion, in this case one can not speak of 'compensated Houses' – as we shall see later, the occupation of any of the other eleven Houses give positive results (i.e. the ones you would expect from a Sun in the 2nd, 3rd, 4th and so on). There is no possible angle of oscillation.

If anything, a possible evidence of the presence of the Sun in a First House can be found by asking the native whether some of his or her close blood relations (parents, sons or daughters, grandparents, uncles, aunts, nephews and nieces) were born under the sign of Aries. Also you can ask the native whether he or she suffers from certain typical pathologies of the first sign of the Zodiac: mainly headaches, neuralgia of the trigeminal nerve, cervical arthrosis, chronic sinusitis, otitis, and so on. Furthermore I try to observe whether there is any trace of wound, fracture, accident, or burn on his face, forehead, or head.

Sun in the Second House

Just like the following ten Houses of the natal chart yet to be described, there can not be any doubt at all about the Sun being in the second house: there is nothing like 'compensated Houses'. An initial visual inspection of the counselee can address you with considerable certainty to a correct trail; however, your trail should rely on a pre-existing justification. Remember that we are talking of individuals born – presumably and approximately – between 2:00 and 4:00 a.m. Therefore we should not try to detect the features of a natal Sun in the 2nd House if your counselee shows you a birth certificate, confirmed by the memory of his parents, indicating that he was actually born, say, at sunset. I mentioned the structure of the native's body.

A person born with this solar position is usually of very thin physique; nevertheless on the contrary, you can find very massive / dilated / obese natives with the Sun in their natal 2nd House. It must be remembered that there is another possible mistake that you should be careful to avoid at this stage. Do not forget that we are referring to our own age and mostly to European civilization. You would be badly mistaken if you thought you could apply the same patterns to Indians or Eskimos or Nigerians. Everything must be considered within the relatively strict frames of a given social, historical, cultural, and political milieu.

Therefore, probably in less than thirty years this very volume will require a laborious overhaul. But let us stick to our time and especially to Europe and the Western world. Possibly this reasoning may not be so true in the U.S., where the percentage of obese reaches disquieting levels among the population. You can not generalize by claiming that nowadays we are all obese. On the one hand it is true that our diet tends to worsen over time and the uncritical use of *fast food*, sweet snacks and whatever else is on the market, leads our build to take a turn for the worse.

But it is equally true that the culture of *the perfect physique* becomes stronger every new day, together with the myth of the athletic or mannequin-like body. Legions of increasingly large population undergo great sacrifices to remain within those limits of body weight that is generally considered to be 'regular'. So, if we accept the notion that one can not generalize, we must also admit that any human being who appears to be particularly thin or 'fleshy' is quite distinguishable from all the others. In this situation, it is almost always that the thyroid or an unsolved problem of orality is involved (see my *Nuova guida all'astrologia*, published by Armenia).

The thinness of a person born with the Sun in the Second House is quite similar to that of natives of the Taurus. In fact, how could you not detect an absolutely evident common features in celebrities like the Italian journalist Indro Montanelli, the Nobel laureate Rita Levi Montalcini, the actress Audrey Hepburn or the Hollywood star Fred Aistare? Or, on the other side, in natives such as Orson Welles, Gino Cervi, Jean Gabin and Senta Berger? Your research shall begin with trying to see if there are other natives of Taurus in the counselee's family. If so, this will be an important clue – and as they say, *three clues are a piece of evidence…* Then, more directly, I will ask, "Do you suffer from throat ache periodically?" Here a good number of people lie, minimize or simply obfuscate. Thus it is a good thing to ply the native with direct questions that can not be circumvented, such as: "Have you ever had your tonsils removed?", "Do you often suffer from colds affecting your throat?", "Are you hoarse from time to time?", "Have you ever had problems at your vocal folds?", "Have you a sore throat often?", "Have you thyroid nodules or altered metabolic values?" Some people lie because they are convinced that the reason of their frequent sore throat does not rely on astrology.

Thus they would answer, "Yes, I told you that I don't suffer in my throat, this is true. But the fact is that my throat suffers simply because I smoke a lot." Sometimes all the answers of an individual to the afore listed questions are negative. If so, I ask, especially of female natives, "In times of major stress in your life or of great sorrow, have you ever experienced moments of lesser bulimia or slight anorexia? In other words, are there periods during which you tend to eat excessively or in which you simply find no interest in food?" Now if you wish to get the correct answer, remember to use adjectives and nouns with care.

Never ask a person if he/she is bulimic, while it is certainly preferable to ask whether, in *rare* periods of his or her life, he/she had experienced excessive behaviour in connection with food... Two thousand years ago nutrition and food were the basis and the fundamental substance of survival. Then the relation between the Second House and food was much closer than in our days. In our days, survival also means owning a home air conditioning, electricity, computers and TV: in a word – *money*. Generally speaking, who has the Sun in the Second House may show two polar attitudes.

He may be very moderate, we can even say greedy; or he may be a spendthrift. In either case he needs the money: so much that he could even get to make it the main reason of his life. Surely, natives with the Sun in the 2nd House consider with great concern the dangerous possibility of not having enough means of subsistence for themselves and for their loved ones in their future old age. Virtually in every case, natives with this position of the natal Sun appear to be fully concerned with this anxiety. They admit it to everybody with surprising naturalness, while their acquaintances seem to find nothing objectionable or reproachable in their concern.

Still in connection with money, we'll be able to detect a relatively large number of people who work in close contact with money, such as cashiers in banks or pubs and everyone else who – for one reason or another – is involved in reckoning and carrying of heavy bundles of banknotes. To those people in fact, tapping money gives them a sort of artificial security that they need anyway...

The throat should also be seen in a positive way. It inevitably leads us to singing and music. Plenty of times I have been able to detect with absolute certainty the position of Sun in this House also when, after many denying answers to my questions, the native confessed, "My hobby is singing in a chorus." Would you ever attribute it to a natal Sun in the First or in the Third House? Let us stress once again that the *libido*, which is the mental direction of a subject, is far more important than the solar-sign nature of the native.

First of all the individual's *libido* is given by the position of his natal Sun in the Houses, and at a second stage by a possible natal *stellium* in the Houses. Thus, as far as singing or music are concerned, you should not be surprised to find out that those considered to be the greatest singers of history – namely Enrico Caruso and Frank Sinatra, the former a native of Pisces and the latter that of Sagittarius – had both the Sun in their Second House. Certified, first class Taurus natives are other great singers like Barbra Streisand and Massimo Ranieri. But even on this particular point, you should be careful in your questioning. For I know a very good writer who has never been enrolled at a chorus; he never sings in public, except on one occasion: when he is at the restaurant with friends and, upon their request, he starts singing.

Then he is able to enchant all those present with beautiful arias from famous operas or classical Neapolitan songs, with a really wonderful voice! A beautiful, warm or at least interesting voice may also lead the native to the profession of dubber, radio speaker, disk jockey and the like. Many actors owe their professional fortune to the interesting voice that they received as a gift at birth.

Thus we come to another interesting and important clue: smell. Smell, in positive and negative, marks a lot of people born with the Sun in the radix Second House. Often you can feel it immediately, even fulminantly: the counselee arrives late and running, say for example in the summer – and his perspiration is quite strong and unpleasant. Especially if the native is female, her smell may represent a sort of strong sexual attraction, similar to the *oestrus* in the animal world. A woman with strong values of Taurus or a special occupation of her Second House is usually a very feminine and sensual individual, who expresses this feature through a skin smell that 'attracts the preys'. Nonetheless the very same smell that normally represents a positive value may end up by becoming damaging when the native (as I told you before) has a moment of stress, panic, or agitation. However, all these natives adore smells – especially the natural fragrances of the freshly wet grass, of the dew, of the barns, of the country farms, and so on... Moreover, they almost always have a great passion for perfumes and the perfumeries – in fact many of them actually own a perfumery. They have a very sensitive nose. They can not stand people who give off bad odours. Concerning this point you will almost always have unconditional confirmation from your counselees.

The relationship between them and the countryside is very strong. In the current context, you will find among them lawyers, doctors, journalists, entrepreneurs and virtually every sort of professional aspiring to retire in the country, for example in a farm-house. Even if the countryside does not belong to the interests of the native, you'll be able to find that he confesses a very strong attraction for nature: sea or mountains.

This brings us to the notion of image, look, photography, cinema, theatre, graphics, design, and the like. This is certainly one of the greatest discoveries that the late lamented Lisa Morpurgo left as a legacy to us. However, 'image' should not be confused with 'visual perception', especially in the pathological sense of the thing. In fact, I could prove it with thousands of concrete examples that the latter has much to do with the axis of the Twelfth / Sixth House and with the signs of Pisces and Virgo. In connection with this specific subject I came often at odds with those colleagues who follow of Lisa Morpurgo's school of thought, who – perhaps – consider this issue as an expression of *lese majesty*. Indeed here, as elsewhere, it is not a matter of competition: our interest is merely scientific, in the broadest sense of the word.

But this is not the right forum for that discussion. Those who want to believe that the diseases affecting the eyes are connected with the Second House are free to do so without me trying to convince them otherwise. Back to 'image' then. Here the evidence is overwhelming, but – as always – we may come across a long wall of more or less conscious denials. So we must proceed with very direct questions such as: "Have you ever been an amateur photographer?"; "Have you ever worked in a darkroom?"; "When you were a child or a girl did they take a lot of pictures of you?"; "As a child or a young person, have you ever acted as an amateur in theatre?"; "Have you ever be enrolled in an acting studio?"; "Have you ever performed as a constant presence, maybe for a limited period, on television?"; "Did your picture appear often in newspapers?

Has it ever been used in advertising?"; "Do you love painting or drawing?"; "Have you anything to do with computer graphics?"; "Do people claim that you are very photogenic?"; "Do you love shooting documentaries? Do you often use the camera?" We could go on for a while, but let us make an example of what I am saying. A lady arrives for counselling and answers with a barrage of *"No!"* to all the questions that I have listed before. So I accept her version and consider that she may be born with the Sun in the Third House. A few months later she makes a new appointment with me. As a gift, she fetches a book published with a cover made from a photograph of beautiful wild woods. It came out this way that her passion was, indeed, photography; but she felt that this was not important because she dealt with that activity exclusively for recreation.

Of course, year after year experience will teach you to be smarter than Sherlock Holmes in your questioning. Thus you will be able to 'compel' your counselees to tell you the truth.

Another very significant attribute in people with the Sun in the second is almost always a love for natural and solid wood. In fact, many natives furnish their home with wood, some of them even come to create or mount the furniture with their own hands.

So, as you surely understand, after such an aimed questioning it is highly unlikely that you may confuse a Sun in the Second House with a Sun in the First or Third House!

Sun in the Third House

Having to detect whether the native's Sun lies in the 2nd, 3rd, or 4th House, the first question that you should ask to yourself in this case is the following: "Is it basically a sedentary or a mobile individual?" In fact, at least from this point of view, there should be no doubt: a person born with fundamentally Taurus-like values (Sun in the Second House) or with predominantly Cancerine values (Sun in the Fourth House) may love everything except mobility.

Conversely, if the native was effectively born with his Sun located in the Third House of birth, he can be considered to be a Gemini to all intents and purposes. And as a Gemini, he or she will be seen to completely possess all the features of *quicksilver* – which precisely typifies those born with the Sun in the 3rd House. Remember though: mobility can be either physical and/or mental. In that, the degree of education of the native and also his profession surely play a considerable role. For example, say that you are trying to rectify the time of birth of a craftsman. Without any prejudice (because you would expand the question soon), you should begin the interview by asking if he loves cars and especially sitting personally behind the wheel. In 99% of cases, you will hit the bull's eye.

Of course, here too you must be careful when listening to the (voluntary or involuntary) false responses of your counselee. He may claim, "No, I am not interested in cars – not at all!" You should ask then, "Tell me; in your life have you driven more or less than 100,000 miles?" He might answer, "One hundred thousand? In my life? Are you kidding? I can drive 100,000 miles in just one year!" Once again I would like to point out that the position of the Sun in the Houses does not inform you about the aspirations, the projects, the waters that the native would have wanted to sail (this sort of references may apply to the Moon instead, rather than to the Sun). The Sun sets a sort of 'seal' revealing in a very reliable way what one really does, rather than what he 'would like to do'. So, as a check to your questions, you necessarily need to detect facts and not expectations.

Say that John Smith spoils a good number of vehicles because he misuses them, driving as if in a permanent F1 race. It does not matter, then, if he claims that when he drives he is sick at heart. He drives much and this is what counts – the rest is a mere abstraction. Another possible question & answer may be: "Do you own a car of some value?" "Yes, I have a Mercedes, but only because I want to travel more safely…" As in many other cases, in this case too you have an obligation to be critical in the most Virgo-like sense of the term. You should therefore reflect: does an individual who may be able to spend 50,000 Euros to buy a car actually behave so for his own physical safety? Would not he spend so much only because he likes his 'toy' very much? And to get it, doesn't he give up much more important things? Everything is relative, of course; but the astrologer is not a computer.

His long experience, even more than his professional skill, is what can show him with certain objectivity, whether the individual he is interviewing is a fan of cars and travels or not. As recently as yesterday (I'm writing this chapter in mid-September 2002), a hairdresser who was sinking fast into debts told me that whenever he could he sat down behind the wheel of his brand-new beautiful car and found great satisfaction in driving from Naples to Brescia or Naples to Trento.

Let us make a digression. I just wrote about *objectivity* in the astrologer's view. It is obvious that objectivity does not exist. But it is also true that people who have been (like me) doing analysis for many years certainly have more than one string to their bow, which can help them more as compared to those who do not know and can not defend themselves from the mechanisms of *psychological projection*. I think – and I have always declared it – that if you wish to play such a delicate role with people (I mean the practical astrologer), together with having a good knowledge of psychology, it would be very helpful if you had undergone a long-lasting depth analysis, exactly to avoid getting hold of the wrong end of the stick..

The digression is over; let us stick to the Sun in the 3rd House.

Do not think you have made a blunder only because your counselee answers you like this: "I do not even have a driver's license!" In fact he might be one of those persons for whom commuting has been a constant experience for long periods of his life. For example, he may be an employee or a teacher who travels forty / fifty miles a day by train from home to work and back. The Sun in the 3rd House may also mark people who have travelled all their life, by boat or hydrofoil, perhaps because their partner or their beloved one lived at the other side of the lake or of the gulf. Remember: to our purposes it is not important the motivation given by the native to justify a specific reality – it is reality itself. Physical mobility may also relate to issues that have nothing to do with transportation. Many times the native seems to be a 'spinning top' in perpetual motion. Perhaps, he is able to clock up a lot of mileage while remaining behind the counter of a pharmacy. However in this case, if the counselee is as critical as the counsellor, the latter may be able to argue, "This may refer to all the traders in a store, may not it?" If we put it this way, the answer cannot but be *Yes*, but – of course – it is necessary to draw a distinction. Ask, for example, "When you travel by train or plane, do you usually spend most of your time sitting or going back and forth in the vehicle?" Even in this case a native may lie, but you should be ready to observe him in detail: is he sitting still on the chair, or does he stir constantly moving hands, arms, legs and feet? If the resulting impression is of someone whose veins or muscles are crossed by electric current, this is a good clue for the hypothesis.

Mobility can also be mental. Those who have strong Geminian elements or the Sun in their Third House are able to accomplish *multitasking*, i.e.

they are capable of performing multiple tasks simultaneously, by means of an extraordinary mental mobility. In the words of my friend Peter Van Wood, only a Gemini (or those born with the Sun in the Third House, I might add) can fry two eggs while reading the newspaper *and* listening to the radio *and* exchange a few jokes with his wife who's in another room. Usually the greed of these people, at a mental level, has really no boundaries. They read everything from novels to essays, from daily paper to weekly magazines. In the absence of anything else, they would even read the phone book... This is very true, of course, for people of a medium-high education, and a little less for others.

Those who went to high school, or at least have a good culture, would read a lot for a lifetime. They would read and study and write. Thus, many of your questions should be aimed in this direction, helping you to focus on a reality like this: "Do you write poems?", "How many?", "Do you write a diary?", "Every day?", "When did you start?" It goes without saying that you should not be interested at all in the occasional actions of the native. Focus only on those actions that have a character of constancy or, at least, those that have lasted for a long period of his life. In this regard I recall once again that your interrogation will surely give better results if it is addressed to a senior instead of a young man. In fact, for the latter everything is a 'potential' but up to that time he might have lived only one-tenth of his own destiny.

Mobility is not exactly synonymous with *communication*, but in our case it may be so. Often the two things are closely intertwined. We can find a large number of representatives, brokers, salespersons and those involved with public relations who have the Sun in the Third House. This is because such work allows them to move constantly and to come in daily contact with new people. Psychology, as we know, basically uses the same tools of astrology: symbols. So, if we were to help an entrepreneur to choose a good sales representative, our first step would be to select subjects born with the Sun in Third House. However, a psychologist would select the candidates by asking them to choose one of these symbols: a circle, a square, a star.

Easily enough, it appears clear that those who choose the square or the circle (closed symbols: desire for protection, the idea of the fort) are not suitable for such work, as opposed to those who choose the star (a symbol of centrifugal projection). If a persons loves mobile phones and regularly answers two or three calls at a time on different phones, would you think that he was born with strong elements in the sign of Cancer (such as the Sun in the Fourth House)?

Starting from this premise, you would proceed by asking, "Given the choice, especially at night, do you prefer to stay home or to go out?" Many times the answer we receive is, "It depends…" Do not let yourself be misled. As I mentioned, you should not care for the native's passionate statements even if he swears on his honour: always stick to the facts. "I *would like* to stay at home, but my wife forces me to go out every night." Do you really think that if the native sitting in front of you were a Cancerian, would you believe that a true Cancerian (with the Sun in the Fourth House) would bear such a torture for more than a few months? Obviously what you should really be interested in wanting to know is, compared to the entire life of the native, how many times or what percentage of it, he stays at home or goes out at night. Believe me, there is little chance to be mistaken if you put it this way.

Besides all that I listed above, in general the Sun in the 3rd House also applies to inveterate smokers: only chimneys of the steel industry (which, as you may know, can never be extinguished) can smoke more than such individuals! The reader will forgive me if I repeat myself, but I have to stress that everything I write in this section is valid in the western world and for the years in which I am writing. Spittoons in trains and public places were an accepted practice in the Wild West of the United States at the end of the nineteenth century, but today people would be horrified at the mere thought of their return. Similarly, we can appreciate that now it is completely (or almost) normal that two women, within an hour of the clock, may be capable of filling our lungs with the smoke of a dozen of cigarettes. Perhaps in a not too distant future, maybe in twenty years from now, smoking women may risk capital punishment for that – similar to those Afghan women who risked death if seen outdoors without their *burqa* no later than in 2001.

Obviously, the character of a person in front of you should also conform with facts, and not just in theory, that he also suffers from a real and dominant disease of the respiratory tract and/or a continued weakness against flu and bronchitis, not to mention being prone to possible attacks of pneumonia in his life, until the day of the interview.

If one or more close blood-relatives of the native were born under the sign of Gemini, your hypothesis of him being born with the Sun in the 3rd House would be strengthened enormously.

Also the visual-objective examination of the native will lead you further toward the placement of the Sun in the Third House or to the exclusion of it. Gemini (but above all: people who have the Sun in the Third house) usually appear very young in body and mind, showing – in most cases – to have fewer years than the age actually recorded on their identity papers. Their eyes are very bright and the whole aspect resembles a *scugnizzo*: the classic Neapolitan 'street urchin' who is unexpectedly cunning and intelligent.

In this connection I remember an episode from the life of the Neapolitan writer and engineer Luciano De Crescenzo (when he used to work at IBM headquarters in Naples). It was mid-July. He had just finished lunch and he was sipping coffee together with representatives of the American multinational company at one of the tables of the bars on the seafront of Mergellina. The heat was stifling and stomachs felt heavy in the post-lunch period, inflicting a sort of narcosis to the party. Suddenly before them appeared a group of street urchins between ten and twelve years of age. They were wet in their bathing suit. They were coming from the nearby beach of the fishermen, next to the mooring of the yachts. The smarter and cleverest among them noticed the drinks bill and the money on the table of their intended victims.

In a split second he assessed the situation and commented, "How much do you give me if I don't take the money and run away?" The writer replied, "A good kick at your backside, if you do not go now." "Really? And when do you reach me if you do not have even the strength to leave your chair?" To make a long story short, for the sake of sympathy, eventually the 'Milanese' [1] handed over one thousand Liras to the insolent but likeable boy.

Due to his own mobility and his attitude for the *multitasking* function mode to which I was referring to earlier, if he really has the Sun in the Third house your counselee will be living his session with the astrologer in any way except than passively. He would unceasingly ask questions. He would hop from one subject to another. He would always interrupt you. He would be intolerant to any long explanation... All this can not be the behaviour of a typical Taurean or Cancerian. The native's superficiality – which is not a negative value, but a means to feed his curiosity about thousands of different subjects – will be evident even to the least attentive among my colleagues!

Also the Sun in Third house, like all other positions, will have its own specific uniqueness in terms of a destiny. It should indicate that a brother or a sister plays a particularly important role in the native's life, a role that can be either positive or negative. So you should ask him several questions about his brothers and sisters, and also about his grandchildren, brothers-in-law, uncles and aunts… I am sure that something important will certainly come out. It may be a famous brother or sister who marked the native's life very positively.

But it could also be serious problems with one of these close relatives, at such a level that has changed his entire life, twisting it towards a specific direction and forever. Sometimes it is also a terrible tragedy. Maybe one of his relatives died young, committed suicide or was seriously injured in a car accident. Other times a natal Sun in the 3rd House may indicate that one of the native's relatives suffers or had suffered from serious mental illness or addiction. In short, when questioning the counselee it is a good thing to propose to him/her a wide range of similar possible situations. What is certain is that one of these close relatives, for better or for worse, has marked or is still marking strongly the life of the person whose natal chart you are trying to rectify.

If I wanted, I could go and write a whole book just on this paragraph. But I think I have offered so many elements that it will be really hard for you not being able to recognize a native of this category.

Sun in the Fourth House

There are really numerous references that may allow you to understand, without undue effort, the exact location of a Sun within the cusps of a House. In terms of *libido*, the 4th House constellates the meanings of the mythologem of the Great Mother. In order to explain what it is, we must first explain what a mythologem is. It is a kind of archetype: something that, at a symbolic level, pre-exists in man.

I would like to explain it better by borrowing an example taken from *Che cos'è la psicologia [What psychology is]*, a book edited in Italy by Biblioteca Universale Rizzoli written by Pierre Daco. Popularizing psychology, the author depicts the following suggesting image. Say that you are in a forest at night, in a night of new moon, very deep inside a totally dark and dense forest. What do you think would be the first thing you'd long for in these circumstances? Do you think it's the light from the sun? Correct! Now take a moment to consider whether that desire is about you in particular or if it doesn't refer instead to the whole of humanity of any historical era, of whatever race or religion, of any social-cultural-economic status, males and females, young and old and so on. What Pierre Daco wanted to demonstrate with that example is the nature of the Sun as an archetype: the archetype of light, heat, safety, strength, joy... While the *mythologem of the Great Mother*, to be precise, can be defined as a sort of acute nostalgia that any native with the Sun in the 4th House feels. They tend to look constantly back to their prenatal life: a wonderful stage that they still wish it could happen once again; a period in which they felt sheltered from everything – changes of temperature, light, noise… Those who live this mythologem, they will always be looking for protective situations throughout their lives: kind of an ideal umbrella under which they would go and repair to gain some condition of stability and regularity, permanence, physical and mental rest. And on the contrary, they would have great difficulty in cutting their own umbilical cord and getting rid of their own mother – of course I am not talking of the physical mother, but of the mother in her symbolic implications.

These individuals avoid all the situations of anxiety, particularly those that can be detrimental to their own stability. They would try to become an employee hired with an open-ended contract, rather than performing any freelance, part-time or interim activity. They would hardly divorce. It is improbable that they would leave their natal home or country. In literature there is an example which reflects this condition very clearly. I refer to Alessandro Baricco's novel, *Novecento* [2]. It's the story of a foundling born in January 1900, hence named *1900* by the crew (who would then adopt him) of the four stacker liner where he was found after being abandoned by the mother. The child grows up in the ocean between two continents, and the boat is like a womb within which he seeks protection.

He would never want to disembark on that land from which he fears, as if it were the gaping jaws of a monster. Even in the end, as an adult, when he is ordered to abandon the ship because it would be destroyed with dynamite because of its aging, the protagonist of the novel prefers to hide in the boat's 'bowels' and die together with the only home he has known, rather than leaving the past behind and starting afresh, landing, and facing real life.

Even in Piero Chiara's novel *La stanza del vescovo* there is a similar character sailing on the lake with his boat: he always keeps at the centre of the lake, away from the dry land, living on the lake as if it were an island.

Let us step back a few thousand years to stress that even the astrologers of many centuries ago noticed that those born in the two hours before midnight, had a predilection for two kinds of activities: on the one hand, those relating to obstetrics and gynaecology, or on the other hand, those relating to architecture, buildings, furnishing. They noticed the connection but were unable to explain it. Then, two centuries ago Sigmund Freud explained that among female genitalia, the uterus is the organ intended to receive the fertilized egg, but the womb is also home. That's why those born with the Sun in the Fourth house love the house regardless of their profession: although the aptest job for them is being a gynaecologist, a midwife, a builder, an estate agent, an architect, an interior designer, and so on.

I know notaries, dentists, mechanics and professionals of every category who every day expedite their work very quickly to run home, where a sort of building site is open indefinitely: there they work relentlessly, adorning the house, changing the furniture, repainting all the time. In short, they love their house; they would not ever give up an evening at home, with some good music or a book or with friends, for anything in the world – not even for a trip to Japan.

You would ask those people, "Do you spend evenings at home or do you rather go out?" "It depends…" "OK, say every hundred days, how many times do you go out at night?" "I'd say ten..." – If he answers so, there can be no doubt about his Sun being in the Fourth House.

Once I met an engineer with strong indications of the sign Cancer. He worked in a huge but closed hall, just like in an enormous box. This was not enough for him: inside the room, he had built a sort of a glass house where he entered every morning and from which he went out only to go back home.

Whatever their field of study or their profession, many people with the Sun in the 4th House spend most of their lives to administer real estate. They like to have relationships with tenants, and with the carpenters whom they call often because they have always something to repair in one of their apartments; they would manage bills, receipts, and contracts and so on. If the person sitting in front of you does something like this, and he does it almost full time, his natal Sun is certainly in the Fourth House.

The properties they deal with may include the restaurant business, hotels or cottages with Bed & Breakfast.

In them, the love for home goes hand in hand with the love for their own places of origin. Many of those born with the Sun in the 4th House are appreciated experts of history and traditions of their hometowns. History, being strongly tied to the past (intrauterine life) 'infects' many of those born between 10 pm and midnight.

Virtually in every case, the computer is another distinctive feature of these people. Computer means memory – Who can be fascinated by memory more than a Cancerian? Usually those who have the natal Sun in the 4th House deal somewhat with computers and computerized information: even if they are writers or historians or professors of philosophy.

Being sedentary, especially physical so, has to be one of the key elements to guide you.

Your ability to detect a Sun in the 4th House significantly increases if there are people born in the sign of Cancer in the counselee's family.

Many times the face of a Cancerian is very easy to spot: it somehow resembles an owl, usually wearing heavily or exaggeratedly rimmed spectacles, as in the case of Cesare Romiti (of course in ten years also this detail may no longer be valid).

Even a pronounced abdomen or breast may help you in recognizing a native with the Sun in the 4th House.

So, once again one might well say that, with the right questions of the interrogation, you would hardly mistake a Sun in the 4th House with a Sun in the 3rd or in the 5th one.

Sun in the Fifth House

If your counselee goes out very often at evening or at night, you can be quite confident that his/her natal Sun lies in the 5th House. Those who see daylight for the first time in hours that are usually between 8 to 10 pm – that is to say, in that time frame which man usually devotes to leisure (cinema, theatre, dance, dining out, love, concerts and so on) – later on as an adult, in 90% of the cases they would feel a strong attraction towards those same activities.

Among this group you will find people who would never give up playing poker at night with friends; they would never renounce a stroll with friends or going out to dinner with boyfriends or girlfriends or to the cinema, theatre, and so on. For those people, having fun every evening is a kind of must. If they stay at home for more than two or three nights in a row they feel they are in jail! So, this first element alone should not leave you the least doubt.

But if you do, here are the other factors you should consider. In many cases, even the native's profession follows such predisposition indicated by the sort of *libido* we are talking about. A native with the Sun in the 5th House would probably be an actor or a director, a scriptwriter or a musician, a dancer or a singer, a professional gambler, a professional athlete – consider that nowadays sport is a show rather than a passion for gyms. Sun in this House also creates animators of holiday villages, managers of cinemas or ballroom dances, in a word a person who lives what may already be considered as the leading international industry – leisure.

Remember though: the 5th House is also the House of children. Therefore it produces many teachers or people who in some way devote themselves to young people. If, for example, a native of this group was born with strongly prevailing values of the sign of Leo, he or she would surely deal with young people in connection to the show business. If the sign of Pisces prevails in his natal chart, he would deal with young people in relation to medical care and so on...

Many times I have seen mothers who were also celebrities in the fields of culture, business, science, etc... but above all they were mothers whose only light was represented by their children.

Other natives with the Sun in the 5th House perennially think of love. Both male and female natives would be a sort of a Don Juan, obsessed almost exclusively on 'hunting'. Their ambition is placing as many flags as possible in their personal map, each one corresponding to an adventure of perhaps one night only.

I mentioned earlier that the predilection for games is very much present (in high percentages) in these natives. Nonetheless you should not forget that *game* is not only represented by cards or roulette. In my life, I have known lots of people with the Sun in the Fifth House, who had never even touched playing cards: but they played with their lives and destinies with the very same strategies of a player at a gambling table. They were people who risked everything and at all times; who were simply unable to put a full stop in their lives. Instead, they indulged in useless and highly risky business ventures.

Sun in the Sixth House

This House shows a lot of interesting and strongly denoted features. After years of fascinating studies, I became convinced that some of the features of the 6th House, not precisely falling within the frame of astrological Tradition, yet greatly enrich and complete its range of meanings. I think that a starting point should be the following basic piece of information: the Sun in the Sixth House aims the native's *libido* towards the body. This granted, it may take four basic directions, although in some cases it is also possible that the native fully or partly *constellates* more than one of the meanings that I am going to elaborate.

The native could be spurred by a relevant interest in other people's bodies, in the medical sense of the thing. If so, he would certainly be a very good doctor, maybe a psychologist, a psychiatrist, a surgeon, a dentist; but he could also perform some paramedical activity, such as physiotherapy, Shiatsu, Reiki; or be a professional nurse, charge nurse and so on. In the second case, the fundamental interest in the bodies of others shown by the native would be in the aesthetic sense of the term. If so, he would be attracted by gymnastics or athletics. He might be a teacher of physical education, the owner of a gym club or of a beauty centre.

Maybe he would be a professional hairdresser, a make-up artist and so on. On the contrary, if the counselee sitting before you shows a sharp tendency for dealing with his/her own body in an aesthetic way, what you would see is a sort of picture of someone who has just come out from the hairdresser's of from a beauty salon. Not a single hair would be out of place. Every square inch of the counselee, borders on a manic obsession for ordered aesthetics.

His hair would be very clean and tidy. He would not leave home without taking a shower, even if he has a temperature of 38°C! Also the aesthetics and tidiness of his clothes, shoes, watch strap and all the rest of his garments would be close to perfection. In this respect, remember that Giacomo Casanova was born with the Sun in the 6th House, and he shaved three times a day! Finally we must consider the hypothesis that the native you are dealing with is highly interested in the care of his/her own body from the medical point of view. The case is a bit more serious, with evident signs of hypochondria that the native expresses by frequent visits to doctors, continuous blood tests, reading encyclopaedias and various medical publications, talking very often about this sort of things, and so on. In his stay in Paris, Frédéric Chopin use to keep his wardrobe full of medications; his health was cared by fourteen doctors! As I wrote above, it is quite possible that your native shows more than one of these attitudes at the same time. For example he may be a hypochondriac doctor. However, in each of the four cases described it will be very easy for you to detect the stigmata of the Sun in the 6th House.

Another fundamental aspect that concerns these natives is their particular skill in the use of hands. But as always, also in this case the native would often deny: "Have you ever given Shiatsu massage?" "No" "Do you always enjoy covering your body with creams?" "No" "Have you ever played the guitar or the piano?" "No" "Do you like crocheting, embroidering, making repairs at home, building anything with wood, repairing watches or doing anything like this?" "No" "Do you enjoy cooking, and particularly preparing with your own hands the dough for cakes or pasta?" "No" "Do you like playing cards?" "Yes… but only because, you see, every night I second my wife who is a passionate player."

OK, let us focus on this for a moment. First of all, you should note that many card players enjoy playing cards because they actually like to *touch* the cards. Those who were born with the Sun in the Sixth House belong to this group. Also note that many people try to exclude astrology when they give you an explanation of their prevailing behaviour. Do not care for this; be only concerned in understanding what the native's prevailing, continuous activity is.

If your counselee really has the Sun in the 6th House, he will be an attentive listener and observer. He would not miss a single word or expression of your face or movement of your hands. This for the simple reason that, being a 'Certified, first class Virgo', he has surely developed a strong critical sense and he would soon discover the… design fault in the toy he's playing with.

He would act like Sherlock Holmes, walking around with a magnifying glass in his hand and sticking to the motto: 'Observe, concatenate, deduce.' Probably due to the law of retaliation, it happens that those people (especially when they grow old) develop serious problems of sight – this also refers to people born with the Sun or stellium in the 12th House. Quite often, it is not necessary to wait for their old age – these natives can show evident sight defects even as young people.

Another element that can guide you with a very high degree of verifiability is the native's almost certain status of being *single*. The majority of unmarried people, or people who do not cohabit with anybody, belongs to the axis Virgo/Pisces or to the axis Sixth/Twelfth House.

Also fussiness is a flag that stands high on the head of such natives. If your counselee opens an engagement book in your presence, you'll be able to see that its pages are a masterpiece of engraving, precision, detail, organization, etc… On the other hand, don't feel discouraged if these natives claim that their lives are actually chaotic. This may well be true, but it would not exclude their fussiness in different areas of their lives. For example, they may show the innate tendency to create bullet lists or numbered lists in which, one entry after another, they tick all the items that they have finished off.

Finally, as always, if the native declares to have some next of kin born in the sign of Virgo, or diseases of eyes, hands, and gastrointestinal system, this could represent the final evidence that we are looking for to establish that his natal Sun is in the 6th House.

Sun in the Seventh House

Often, very often, the native with this solar position is sure to have a unique apparent mental direction: love. But with a proper interview you'll realize that the keyword crossing and characterizing all of his/her existence is 'war' in fact. This native is a born warrior; most likely he would be a lawyer or a lieutenant of Police, a policeman, a soldier, an officer of any sort of army, a judge…

On the other hand, this story of love is not completely airy-fairy. This native aspires very strongly to achieve a unique, exclusive, exceptional relationship, such to being launched into the orbit of hyperbolic feelings for which there are not enough adjectives to describe its wonders. By thinking so, those born with the Sun in the 7th House raise exaggerated expectations in love. This may represent a high factor of risk. For example, if such a native invests in the stock market, he might be willing to invest all his savings, say, into shares of a telephone company. If those shares fall, his life would be a disaster as a consequence.

More realistically, you can say that in case of strong emotional disappointment, this native's feelings towards the beloved one can pass from the blindest of love to absolute hatred. However, if you examine the entire span of his life, you will certainly find many more facts of war than love. Proceedings, courts, lawyers or simple personal disputes would dot almost every year of his life. It is almost unthinkable that he hasn't ever been implicated in at least one important court case in the course of his existence. Whether he realizes it or not he is born for war and to act as a lawyer, preferably dealing with criminal cases.

Other times his *libido*, not incorrectly, spur this native to surrogated or non-surrogate forms of this nature. These people usually deal with politics, trade unions, and/or show a strong civil and social commitment. For example, they would be environmental activists, struggling for animal welfare and becoming members of the most radical or passionate associations of this kind (Greenpeace, Hands off Cain, etc.).

In any case, talking about his character, this native is a warmonger, a troublemaker – by conscious or unconscious vocation. Throughout his life, he stands high chances of digging deep ruts around him, thus severing all relationship with his spouse, siblings, sometimes even with his parents, with friends...

He lives the idea of justice in such a strong way that if he sees somebody committing an act of blatant injustice, while others may remain passive or silent he is moved like a sailboat in the fury of the storm and without hesitation, he does something to redress the wrong. Using another metaphor, we can say that he starts like a railway engine – nobody will be able to stop him. Some will say: Is this is not good? It may be, if he only was able to distinguish between justice and justicialism. In the latter case, in a span of time close to zero the native attempts to be prosecutor, judge and executor of the sentence which he pronounced even before the beginning of the case.

The point is that he does not realize that there is something called objective justice which is different from subjective justice. Unfortunately, next to celebrities with a Seventh House full of stars who have proved capable of so much love as the great Saint Pio of Pietrelcina (although even in his life there were major conflicts), history has also produced other natives with a Seventh House full of stars, for whom war was their main *raison d'être* – such as Adolf Hitler and Benito Mussolini.

So, your interview with a counselee potentially born with the Sun in the 7th House shall begin with (personal or not personal) conflicts, causes and wars. In ninety percent of cases, the counselee will deny, in good faith, because he can not simply see the many wars that have accompanied and still accompany his existence. Dwell on his family members. "Has your father or brother or son ever had serious incidents with the law? Perhaps even if they were totally innocent?", "Has your family ever been the subject of a lengthy court case?", "Have you personally ever suffered been involved in bankruptcy, in a trial?", "Have you ever insulted a public officer?", "Perhaps you have been the victim of a miscarriage of justice?" Usually, this latter question helps many people recover their memory.

Even if they are architects or dentists by profession, most of these natives are well-trained in matters of law and politics. Ask them to tell their life summary: you'll find many incurable wounds in their parental relationship or in their friendship. They usually represent irreversible breakaways in their life.

And if it turns out that there are also family members belonging to the sign of Libra, can be quite sure that these natives' Sun is in the 7th House.

In other cases the diseases typical of the native Libra, such as those regarding renal function, emerge from an early age and can enlighten you on the presence of the Sun in this House. As an example, you may notice that the native needs to go to the bathroom very often; or on the contrary, he may go to the toilet very rarely during the entire day.

Sun in the Eighth House

It is usually more easily recognizable in a female than in a male native: in 99% of cases she suffers from gynaecological problems. "No, – she may claim – I never had gynaecological problems." "Not even – you should ask – painful menstruation or amenorrhea (absence of menstruation) or dysmenorrhoea (excessive discharge during menstruation)?" "No" "Not even small uterine or ovary cysts? Maybe myomas?" "No" "Not even lesser sexually transmitted infections such as *candidiasis* or the like?" "Yes, but only sometimes and only because of this and that..." "Have you never had abortions?" "Just a couple..." The native's appearance itself may be sufficient to help us detect Sun in the 8th House.

He/she strongly looks like a native born under the sign of Scorpio: with very dark hair and eyes. He or she usually prefers dark colours; he/she often dresses in black. Male natives also suffer from problems of the genitals, but to a lesser extent: perhaps lesser venereal infections; some of them may have undergone minor surgery for short fraenulum, for example, or to help an undescended testicle into the scrotum. Both men and women born with the Sun in this House often suffer or have suffered from haemorrhoids.

It is also very easy to detect the Scorpionic character in them, even if a native was actually born with the Sun in Libra, Gemini or any other sign of the Zodiac. In almost all of the people born with the Sun in the 8th House, torment appears to be their psychologically dominant leaning, which represents the key word of these natives. Even if from all points of view they could live a regular and serene life, they would always – unconsciously – choose twisted situations, impossible ties, situations of perpetual *pathos*, tensions and general conflicts...

Often death has left its mark heavily on them, directly or indirectly. It may be the early loss of a parent or a close relative, but it may also be that they witnessed – at an early age and with their own eyes – a casualty, or their family was hit by a severe grief, etc.

But in the overwhelming majority of cases, the native themselves or some of their close relatives have suffered serious economic setbacks or other serious financial problems such as bankruptcies, forced sales of property, loss of goods, total or partial loss of savings for bad investments, fraud by friends or relatives, financial 'bleedings' perhaps in order to save a relative from troubles, huge loss of money because of robbery or burglary, postponed inheritance and so on. It is virtually impossible that this latter item of the above list doesn't match reality. Do not be fooled by the apparent or real wealth of the counselee sitting in front of you. I remember a particular episode. In front of me was a luminary of science of international renown. I warned him that he would stand serious chances to lose huge amounts of money, but he laughed at me, "Probably, he thought, he does not know my economic bases." A few years later I saw his picture in the papers. He had lost all his possessions in the collapse of a financial company offering fabulous profits to its current account holders.

If they have chosen their job well, these natives would usually be notaries or archaeologists, geologists or psychologists – because all these professions are somehow related to death, excavations, to what lies 'below'... Other times they would very often be in contact with death, perhaps working as doctors in an intensive care unit or taking care of the terminally ill, for example in voluntary work. And if they have other jobs, then in the overwhelming majority of cases they would be good amateur psychologists.

They have a highly developed sixth sense and certainly psychic powers (extra-sensory perceptions). Female natives would be people who are real witches, capable of telepathic flashes, premonitory dreams, extraordinary intuition... It would be good to teach them how to fulfil their potential. Carl Gustav Jung explained that during the day, each of us may live different significant events that we usually ignore for lack of attention.

The natives born with the Sun in this house would certainly live many more special events than an average person: they should always wonder about the meaning of the symbols in which they continuously run. For example, consider that one morning you wake up and start whistling the song titled *Apple*. During the afternoon you watch a film where you can see apples, several times and in different scenes. After ages that you hadn't heard from him, in the evening you receive a call from a Mr. Apple. Now if you had paid attention to the signs of the day, you would have understood in advance that your old friend, Mr. Apple, would soon let his voice be heard.

Usually these natives are very intelligent people, but have also a troubled and twisted personality. Their life is never easy, because they prefer salty and peppery 'food' to any other 'food' that probably is less harmful, but which is also a bit 'tasteless'.

The presence of natives in the sign of Scorpio in their family can represent a sort of confirmation of the presence of the Sun in their Eighth natal House.

Almost always, the finances of their partners have a decisive (either positive or negative) role in their lives: remember that in the system of derived Houses – which is a really valuable system in astrology – the native's 8th House represents the partner's 2nd House).

Sun in the Ninth House

The Sagittarian values of the Sun in the 9th House usually stand out quite evidently. The native is strongly leaning towards the distant, either in the geographical-spatial or in the metaphysical-transcendental meaning of the term. For the most part the native leaves the former condition in his youth and the latter one with maturity. However, many times the two spin projections proceed almost in parallel since his youth. The native shows a great interest for travel, as well as – usually – the interest for foreign languages, which very often are the very basis of the native's profession. The majority of them are people who have lived abroad or who have been living for long months in other cities or regions in their native country.

Please note that the 9th House in astrology refers to that land where they speak a language or dialect other than the native's own. Even if the native has never lived away from home, this is exactly what he wants to do. Usually at the top of his interests there is the desire to go to live abroad. In the instincts of those born with the Sun in this House you can find etched the most marked pioneer pushes, in the broadest sense that you can imagine. The exploration of new territories, considered also at a mental level, is their main objective. Everything is already inscribed in the graphic symbol of the sign: an arrow shot out and upward. Do not forget that the sign of Sagittarius corresponds to that time of year when farmers, in full winter freeze, sow hoping to gather in the summer. What could be far more optimistically 'far away' than this? If it's born with the sign in the 9th House, your counselee is an example of the ultimate expression of optimism, and therefore the least expression of distrust. From this point of view, we can say that in a way Sagittarius is 'opposed' to Virgo.

In fact, we can say that a Sagittarian naivety or a musketeer-like spirit animates this native. He would rush forward with his foil, not caring if he would be welcomed by a pillow or by a mouth of cannon aiming at him. In the majority of cases his ingenuity is exaggerated: even at eighty years, he would give big slaps on his forehead, exclaiming, "Oh, how could I be so naive?" Representing the very essence of the lack of distrust, these natives are brought to conform to fashion, to imitate trends without any critical sense. The best impersonators belong to this sign. For example, you may happen to be in a party when a couple of times a new noun or verb is pronounced: you will see that if there are Sagittarians there, they would immediately adopt it!

This exaggerated 'jupiterian' presence we are talking about also means that, in many cases, this native is excessive even in their physical expression or in speech (pure logorrhoea!), or in occupying the space of others and so on...

His energy is extraordinary and, many times, he is concerned about sports in terms of pure pleasure or for racing or profession. In the majority of cases these natives also profess a great passion for animals (particularly horses).

I already mentioned languages, but remember that they can be also programming languages.

Of course, the native's physical exuberance depends whether he is more inclined towards the geographical-spatial or the mental-spiritual exploration of a land. In the latter case it may be an apparently hypotensive person, whose phlegm mainly relies on his diet (without meat, smoke, alcohol, etc.) and meditation. In any case you can notice different forms of exaggerated love for everything that comes from abroad: garments, literature, cars and so on.

In many cases, the native's liver is compromised and a confirmation of this is much more than a clue. Also in the field of love, almost always it's people who look away, geographically speaking.

There will be a great help to know if they have close relatives born under the sign of Sagittarius.

Another very interesting element has to do with traffic accidents. In the overwhelming majority of cases, the natives themselves or one of their close relatives have been victims of a serious accident. Perhaps an accident in which they may not have reported injuries, but in which a car was destroyed.

The comparison, as in all other cases, should be made considering whether the counselee could belong to one of the neighbouring signs: in this case, a Scorpio or a Capricorn. Could you ever mistake a dark Scorpio for Sagittarius? Or for a Capricorn? Could a Capricorn, one who appears to have swallowed a billiard cue because of his deep care for an upright posture, ever be mistaken for a naive, optimistic and a bit gaffer of a Sagittarius?

Sun in the Tenth House

It is relatively easy to detect a Sun in the Tenth House, for it corresponds to natives with very strong features of Capricorn. These people usually have a critical need for pleasure, either at physical or (much more frequently) at an intellectual / cultural / professional level. Their need is mainly reflected in the special care that they devote to clothing, to their own *looks*, to their own elegance. Usually these natives wear an abundance of jewellery, typically precious and tastefully chosen. Their posture generally resembles that of a king. Somehow it suggests the idea of someone who has just swallowed a sword or a pool cue and is therefore forced to keep his torso as straight as a plumb line. Still in reference to posture, they also show a constant tension. These natives only rarely relax; it is as if they would not like lose their self-control. Their glance is in perennial interrogation, seemingly looking for your appreciation, your confirmation... Just in case he didn't tell you on the phone, as soon as he arrives this native immediately stresses the fact that he is a doctor, a professor, someone who occupies a relevant position in society, perhaps someone who has two doctorates, who speaks three languages and so on. This is normal and legitimate, but if you notice an unusual precipitation in your counselee giving this sort of information, this is already a clue of the presence of the Sun in his natal 10th House.

It is quite obvious that your interlocutor is perched high up on the business or (more generally speaking) in social ladder. He usually invests an enormous amount of energy to raise his own celebrity, image, position in society. If you ask him for a brief curriculum vitae, it should not be difficult for you to avoid confusion and exclude that his Sun may be located in the 9th or in the 11th House. Virtually in any case, the native shows one absolute imperative: to emerge. It goes without saying that one can emerge even – apparently – in the opposite direction other than the power and the magnification of the *ego*.

Thus, these natives may take on the role of the hermit, detaching themselves from society, embracing asceticism, spirituality... but psychology teaches us that one can also take alternative routes to reach the final goal to be the first in some field. Taking the risk of sounding blasphemous, in describing the characteristics of Capricorn André Barbault wrote that the Christ wanted to be the first in everything: in martyrdom, in endurance, in taking on His shoulders all the sins of the world... And of course it does not matter if Jesus was born on the 25th of December or any other day – we are simply referring to symbols.

The native's huge need for 'a place in the sun' is usually reflected in his faultless professional behaviour. In almost all cases, people born with the Sun in the Tenth House stand out for their professionalism, their dedication to work, their great sense of duty, their Stakhanovism...If you get to know that your counselee is also president of something, then there can no longer be any doubt of him being born with the Sun in the 10th House. In fact Capricorns (or people with the Sun in the Tenth House) consciously or unconsciously work all their lives to take some chair at school, in the Rotary Club, in politics or in a company: it may be headmastership, deanship, chairmanship or even – presidency. What moves this native, as we have said, is not so much money or power itself, but it's rather the need of being praised by others. This native wants to be able to show to everyone, and especially to himself or herself, that he/she is not inferior to anyone.

Moreover, very often, you can detect a very important figure of a mother in their lives (in positive or in negative): a mother who has impressed turns of major importance to their lives.

If there are individuals born in the sign of Capricorn in the native's family, the chances that the latter has the Sun in this House are significantly increased.

And if you detect that the native suffers from any problems with the bones (especially the knee) or the teeth or skin allergies and/or respiratory diseases, all this may offer further confirmation of your hypothesis.

Sun in the Eleventh House

If your counselee was born with the Sun in the 11th House, it is a 'Certified, first class Aquarius'. His (or her) Aquarian features should be visible, evident to everybody. First of all, the native has a great love for music.

So ask, "Do you love music?"

Maybe the reply would be, "No"

"Have you ever played any instrument?"

"No"

"Have you ever sung?"

"No"

"Do you listen to music while working?"

"Sometimes, but this is only because of the fact that..."

Let us focus on this once again. In the overwhelming majority of cases, man tends to think that if he accomplishes something (even something quite specific) this does not depend on the position of the celestials when he was born – it actually depends on current or occasional factors. Maybe this point of view may be explained by a series of psychological repressions, but there could be other reasons.

So let's continue with the interview.

"OK, tell me how many hours, on average, you listen to music."

"Well, let's say that when I am in office, while looking after my paperwork, I have music playing in the background."

Not everybody likes music. Please note that I personally am deeply disturbed by music, whatever activity I am doing.

"Do you listen to music when you drive?"

"Yes, I have a car radio: not to get bored during long journeys, I listen to music."

"Would you be able to say the title of at least one of the songs of the top Italian singers today?"

"I think so, but I think everyone should be able to say this."

Please note that *I* am not able to say this.

"Have you ever purchased music CDs or cassettes or discs?"

"Yes, I have a fairly good number of them."

"Do you ever go to concerts?"

"Sometimes."

"I am not sure I understand. You listen to music almost all day long and also while travelling. You can recognize singers and songs. You buy music CDs and go to concerts. So how can you say that you do not like music?"

Actually, the latter question is a rhetoric, which I usually avoid asking, because after all it does not matter to understand why the native has lied, even if in good faith. What you are interested in establishing, beyond any reasonable doubt, is whether your counselee loves music or not. You can rest assured that if the Sun is in his Tenth house, he would hardly answer like above, unless his birth chart has other very strong elements in Aquarius or Taurus.

But let us proceed. Friendship should represent a great value for these natives; sometimes even more than love itself. But – how can you measure such a variable? There is a way in fact – try to get to know whether the native has maintained good friendly relations with his/her former partners.

Another fundamental point is given by the drive toward originality or eccentricity. You do not have to convince a special 'runaway jury' as in the film based on a novel by John Grisham. If the native is attired in a very original and even eccentric way, you can decide yourself that his Sun in the 11th House – alone and without any show of hands. Once I met an old high school teacher who dressed in red from head to toe, including bag, hat and shoes!

Other times, this native has a very special car, say painted in blue with pink stars. Perhaps he wears two watches on the same wrist and so on. Could you have still doubts? Do you think a Capricorn or a Pisces would do such things?

Real Aquarians do not care for anything and of anybody. *I don't give a damn* was the motto written on the Fascist soldiers' tin hat. A native with the Sun in this House would adopt this motto, regardless of whether he is left-wing or right-wing, an extremist or a moderate. Saying *I don't care* – that is to say, being truly independent and emancipated as only real Aquarians can be – not only means that they do not fear the judgments of others, it also means that the misfortunes apparently slip on them without breaking their heart to pieces. I know an Aquarian who was the protagonist of repeated, billionaire bankruptcies in his life. Because of his failures, not only had he lost his bank accounts, but also his wife, children, home, car and everything else. Nonetheless, if I happened to meet him on the street the day after the failure, I always found him smiling and ready to come up with something to start over and over again.

In the majority of cases the position of the Sun in the Eleventh House also expresses an important death in the native's life.

If in the native's family there are people born in the sign of Aquarius, your track gains in value. This is also true if your counselee suffers from blood circulation problems (e.g. fragility of capillaries or varicose veins), blood pressure or bad hearing. It is incredible to notice that the latter fact has never been detected in five thousand years of astrological observation while the majority of people suffering with hearing troubles *and* born with important elements in Aquarius is overwhelming. And on the other hand, hearing impairment is the most evident somatic effect of people thinking, *"I don't want to hear you."*

And quite often, people with this solar position have outstanding 'bunny-like' front teeth.

Sun in the Twelfth House

Well, I guess that it is virtually impossible not to recognize such a person.

When assessing for Sun in the 12th House, your investigation must necessary start with his/her feet and eyes.

In this regard I would like to recall a very funny episode that happened during the first international congress of astrology held in 1975 in Milan, at the Museum of Science and Technology. I delivered a lecture there along with a very few other international researchers. The room was crowded as never before in other conferences on astrology.

André Barbault was holding his lecture, when a gentleman from the audience asked to speak. He had a scary squint and wore glasses with lenses so thick that they looked like binoculars. Barbault said, "You can speak, but first tell me: are there in your horoscope Pisces sailing crooked?" "Well, I am a Pisces!", replied the gentleman, and the entire audience burst into a loud laughter.

In the majority of cases, the native with the Sun in the 12th House is characterized by a glaring flaw in the eyes such as strabismus, one eye larger than another, eyelids flapping all the time, a spot of a different colour in one of the two eyeballs, etc. Be careful, though, when investigating this detail. If the problem concerns the past, the native is almost never willing to admit it, treating it as if it were an infamous venereal disease...

Everybody would like to say, "I have beautiful eyes" even in the absence of a perfect *silhouette*. so you should play with some 'cunning' and ask, "Hasn't your mother ever told you that in your childhood you had a slight squint? You know, that sort of very light, cute squint like the one of Venus, the goddess?" Perhaps the native would admit, "Oh now that you tell me, yes, I used to have. But then it completely disappeared."

Other times, the interrogation must go on for quite a while before you are able to find that the native underwent eye surgery but he 'had forgotten it', or that as a child he/she was injured or burned in the eyes.

Other times your counselee has ten degrees of myopia despite being only 30 years old, but he claims that this is not a defect because with contact lenses, he can see very well.

Still other times you get to know that the native suffers from a chronic form of pinkeye, or perhaps you find out that the connection with the Sun in the 12th House and his view must be detected at a psychological level, rather than at a level of a real physical disease. In the latter case, the native may be at the head of an association of *Friends of the guide dogs for the blind*. Perhaps he is an ophthalmologist like the protagonist of Woody Allen's *Crimes and Misdemeanors* – an incredible, articulate, repeated, multi-faceted metaphor of life. The film is full of references to sight and view: God's eyes looking at us, rabbis who do not see the reality, ophthalmologists who should treat the blind while they aren't even able to see and so on.

Let's talk about the native's feet. Also in this connection, you could almost never rely on the native's cooperation. He would usually deny any problem with his feet, while eventually admitting that – perhaps – he wears oversized shoes or have flat feet or bunion. Other times the native's peculiar link with feet is more hidden. You would have to dig deeper to eventually find out that he had a fracture in the foot, some ingrown nails, or that perhaps he lost a nail in his life. Perhaps it could be a bad burn at a foot, or he had to wear orthopaedic shoes for three years, or simply the neurotic desire to take the shoes off and walk barefoot as soon as he arrives home. Or maybe the native needs to wear custom-made shoes otherwise the feet hurt. Maybe he walks in a zigzag manner as if he were a sailor just landed from his ship after ten months of constantly being at sea, and so on.

Obviously, the link between the Sun in the 12th House and feet can also be a positive one: the subject may be or may have been a very good dancer, for example.

I think the most sensational case of psychological repression that I happened to experience was the following. After a long series of questions on the above listed, feet-related events, always receiving a flat *No!* for an answer, at the end of the session of counselling I saw my counselee getting up and walking towards the door with a spectacular lameness that I hadn't noticed when he had entered my study.

Within the frame of a possible Sun in this House, another classical point is the native's vocation or spirit of providing nursing assistance. Every native of this group shows this attitude in a very striking way, although they often deny it because they claim that they are *sick at heart* when they have to help others. This may be true.

"Have you ever assisted sick relatives?"

"Once my mother got seriously ill and I had to assist her for a couple of years. But I did it only because I am her only daughter."

"So was it the only time in your life…?"

"No, in fact I had to assist my former partner also, I happened to care for him for a few months."

"When a relative or friend of yours – be he close or distant – lies in hospital, are you usually asked to be with him or with her at night in the hospital?"

"Yes, sometimes it happens, but I do it unwillingly."

This latter answer implies a fundamental bottom line of your interrogation: For astrological purposes, you should not be interested in knowing what the native wants to do, but what he/she *does* in fact. That is the expression of his *libido*, the direction of his Sun. The native's dreams and illusions, the waters that he would have wanted to sail can give indications on the position of his natal Moon, not of the Sun in the twelve Houses!

Nonetheless, in the overwhelming majority of cases the counselee sitting in front of you is usually willing to admit his own vocation of nursing assistance; or at least a very strong spiritual spur. He is also usually able to blurt out a very long list of concrete evidence for it.

If your counselee does so, you would hardly be able to keep on doubting that his Sun is *not* in the 12th house, because such an attitude could be hardly detected in those who were born with the Sun in the 11th House or in the 1st House.

In some cases, these natives are profound scholars, researchers, bookworms, people sitting all day confined in a narrow space to write, read, study and research.

If there isn't any disease affecting his family, there should be some affecting him or her in person, forcing him to take constant care of his own physical or mental health. In this group of people you would find many chronic and serious diseases. Often they were born ill.

In particular, female natives are frequently having to take care of their father first, then their mate and eventually, their son.

From a professional point of view, most of them can be doctors, psychoanalysts, psychologists, social workers, sociologists, nurses, paramedics, prison guards, nuns, monks and so on.

Probably the most spectacular aspect of this solar position is given by a paranoid type of attitude towards life. In a neurotic rather than psychotic way, as time passes by – and every year stronger and stronger – these natives think that life is difficult and that it nurses a grievance against him; that they must defend themselves from everybody and everything; that they should never lower the guard; that diffidence is one of the most positive values in life.

This is why most of these natives are unmarried – they are afraid of being deceived or betrayed by their partners and by life itself.

Very often these people are forced to bear one or more crosses for many years of their existence. Maybe not health-related crosses: for example, they might have to maintain economically a brother, or they might be involved in a similar situation with another close relative. The actual or suspected existence of secret enemies will be the final corollary to this type of investigation.

In conclusion, considering all these clues, I think it's impossible to confuse a Sun in the Twelfth House with a Sun in the First or in the Eleventh House.

Notes
1) Translator's Note: That's how they used to call strangers in Naples.
2) Translator's Note: Giuseppe Tornatore's film The Legend of 1900 is inspired on this novel.

3.
Positioning the 'sensors'

It is a quite a simple technique – it is harder to explain than to do it.

Let's start with the first example. In the year 2000, one of my counselees left to *aim* his SR (ASR) to the Far East. I had studied his case and suggested the ASR shown in figure. As you can see, besides being beautiful in many ways, his ASR had another peculiarity: the Sun played the role of a *sensor* near the Imum Coeli. In fact, Jupiter was clearly placed in the Gauquelin sector – I would have had the opportunity to bring it closer to the MC but I didn't, because I also wanted to *test* the time of birth of the native, to whom I said, "If you were born exactly at the time you mentioned, then this time next year, the Sun of SR would have worked prevailingly in the 3rd House of SR: something special in your relationship with your brothers, sisters, brothers-in love, sisters-in-law, and so on; or perhaps you will buy a news car, or your car will be stolen; or you may start studying a foreign language or something similar. Otherwise the 'headlines' of this SR would talk of one of your parents and of possible habitat issues."

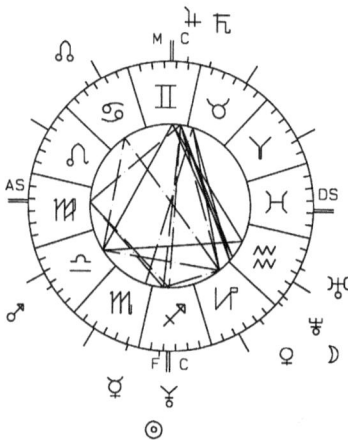

And, in fact, the latter hypothesis proved to be the correct one. He got married, he had a sequel of trivial and significant annoyances due to works in his new home; he experienced troubles in connection with the construction company; and he suffered because of a severe stroke that struck his father.

Considering all these events, I would reasonably infer that his time of birth had to be set back by about fifteen minutes.

In this case, the events of the year were strikingly evident. There could be no doubt, but – unfortunately – it is not always that in the analysis of a year, *a posteriori* allows you to split 'with the knife' similar cuspidal situations. Of course, one sighting or instance of an event does not necessarily indicate a trend. So, you will proceed with further investigation, but this piece of evidence is certainly important in defining, at least on one side, the range of approximation of the native's time of birth.

Case 2

Here is another interesting case: it can help us understand how this method of correction of the time of birth really works. But as I have already mentioned, it should be integrated and not replaced with the other techniques described in this book.

Let us consider the example of a female subject from Campania whose SR chart of 2001 is shown below. As you can see, it has been relocated quite well – in fact, it led to quite satisfactory results. Jupiter at the Midheaven in the Gauquelin sector, as well as a stellium with Venus in the 2nd House, produced – as the lady herself told me – "that final gust of wind that allowed my glider to go beyond the rocky barrier I had in front of me…" To make a long story short, the lady had

overcome a critical period for her small enterprise: almost magically, her turnover had welcomed a good amount of new and significant clients.

But what is interesting here is to stress the position of Mars and Uranus, almost on the edge of the Fifth House. Many years ago, when she first contacted me, the lady told me she was born at 8:00 pm, but starting from the following year, we had always considered a time of birth

rectified to 7:30 pm. In recent years, noting in particular a specific ASR, a doubt arose in my mind that the time had to be retouched backwards for an additional 5-10 minutes. This ASR seemed to be the right opportunity to ascertain this detail. My interview, therefore, started from there. I asked the lady whether during the year of that SR she had completed real estate transactions in property or renovations. At first, her answer was an abrupt *No!*, but it was mere amnesia because immediately after she recalled having purchased some adjacent room to her home, had had it enlarged and several works were made in connection with that extension. I asked for her young child and her husband, but she told me she had had no problem in the twelve months covered by that specific SR. So, at least on the basis of this example, I could begin to infer that Mars had certainly fallen in the Fourth House of that SR, certainly not in the Fifth House.

However, I decided to insist; to detect whether Uranus had fallen in the Fifth. I directed many more questions at the lady, discovering that one of the problems of that specific year was generated by the sudden dismissal of a baby-sitter. This incident had caused to the lady and her husband, the inability to leave for summer holidays and a series of attempts to find a new baby-sitter, who eventually came and lived in the new premises she had recently purchased. All this makes me believe that there is a high probability that Uranus had been in the Fifth House. However, from the point of view of the starting question, this example can not allow a further correction of ten minutes to the already rectified time of birth on which I and that lady have been working for years. In fact, with that time of birth, Uranus was already at less than two and a half degrees from the cusp of the Fifth House (Gauquelin sector) – therefore, it may have acted as either as being in the 5th House or in the 4th House.

However, what this case can say with certainty is that when relocating, you can not go back so as to bring Mars to two and a half degrees away from the cusp of the Fifth House. And this is not a trivial or superfluous piece of information.

Case 3

This is a case of *unwilling positioning* that produced some unintended dramatic results and one wonderful event, thus allowing me to fix in a single stroke – and with a very high level of precision – the time of birth that the counselee had previously provided.

He claimed to be born at 2:00 pm. My first interview had led me to infer that it was certainly an approximate time of birth, although I hadn't been able to determine to what extent. Thinking that it could be rounded up by the usual 15-20 minutes, I had suggested to this native the ASR that you can see in figure: a wonderfully aimed SR that would produce striking effects, to put it mildly.

Nevertheless, twelve months later it turned out that things had gone into effect even more dramatically: his mother had died, he had experienced what we could call a *descent into hell* at an economic and professional level; and had suffered form a subsequent general state of despair.

The only really extraordinary thing of that year had been the following one. He had spent nearly 80% of the year with a newly born love: a very good girl who had surrounded him with all her affection and whose parents proved to be two special parents-in-law – excellent people from any point of view.

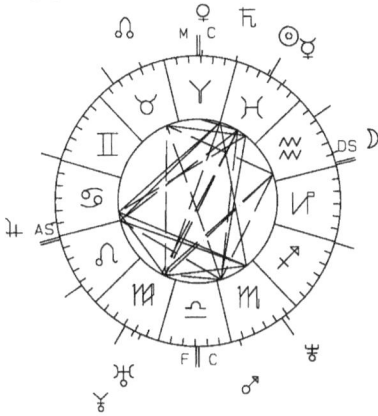

ASR if the time of birth is 2:00 pm

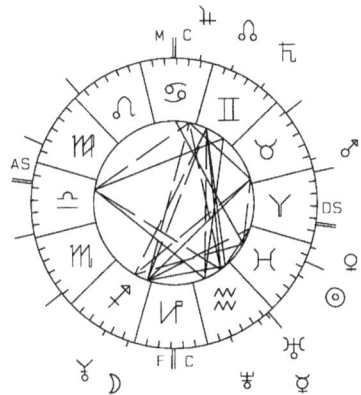

Birth chart, birth time 2:00 pm

Now it is quite clear that the events described above unequivocally indicate that not only the native was born half an hour before his official time of birth (the Sun had certainly occupied the Sixth House, not the Fifth one), but also that, without wishing to boast in any way, the native could have been born *at least* 45 minutes before.

In fact, if it was just a matter of moving the Sun backwards to the Sixth House, we would not need to push back so much in time; while the following three important events suggest that the subject should be born at least 45 minutes before 2 pm:

1) The death of his mother (in this case, the Ascendant of SR moves close to the Imum Coeli of his natal chart).

2) The acquisition of two very wonderful in-laws (the same position as described above).

3) An important love (Venus comes very close to the Descendant).

ASR if the time of birth is 1:15 pm

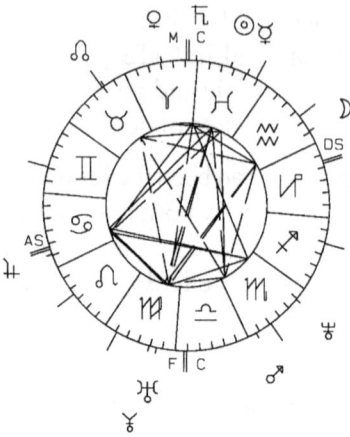

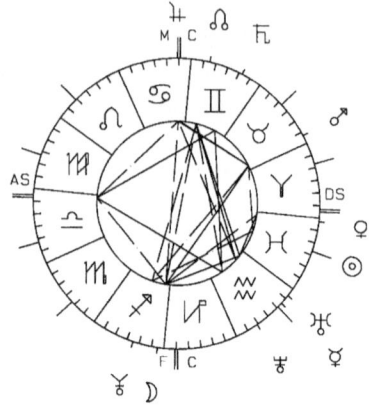

Birth chart, birth time 1:15 pm

It is likely that I will go back further with his time of birth, but this is only a new starting point for my studies. It is also the starting point for attempting, from his next aimed birthday, to give a new, bright professional turning point to my counselee.

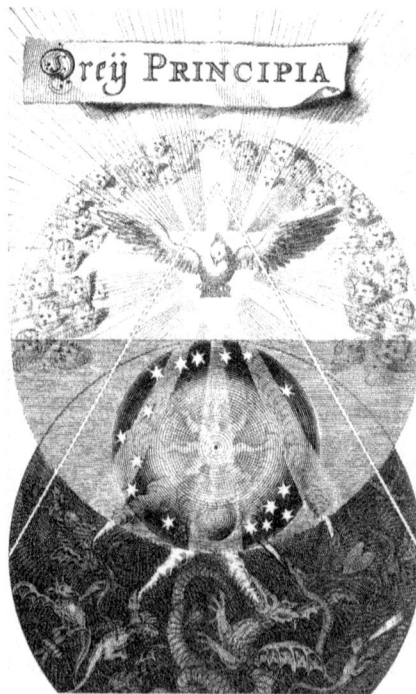

Orey PRINCIPIA

4.
The entrance of Mars in the natal Houses

Why do I suggest you to consider the entrance of Mars in the Houses of birth and not, for example, those of Saturn? For two basic reasons:

1) On an average, transit Mars enters five to six Houses a year, while Saturn passes from one House to another every two or three years. So, if you wanted to consider Saturn, your investigation would continue over many decades.

2) The entrance of Mars in the Houses does not cause nuclear explosions, but it is similar to bee stings. In my experience, the very day of its arrival in a House (or in a span of time starting from two days before and two days after its expected entrance), Mars announces some sharp and clear event.

So, if you proceed by recalling that one sighting or instance of an event does not necessarily indicate a trend, and the more material you collect the better, following a careful study of at least three years of Mars entering the Houses of the natal chart and after the initial *interview* with your counselee, you can reasonably expect that you have collected enough elements to rectify his/her time of birth. Possibly, you could not rectify the time of birth to the minute, but you could certainly correct it within a range of a dozen of minutes – to all intents and purposes it is an approximation that allows you to work safely on that natal chart as well as with the Aimed Solar Returns.

This is how the native himself should proceed.

First of all, you would recommend him to buy an exercise book or a notebook. On the left side of the page he would list, in order, all the entrances of Mars in his natal Houses (based on the ephemerides or with the help of good astrological software) that are computed for the following three years. On the right side he would note how many days before or after the computed entrance, an event (or more than one event) has occurred among those connected with the transit of Mars in each House.

It is important that you explain to the counselee that he shall not let the situation slip out of control and shall not think of having to redo a second draft of *The Betrothed* – because this would undermine the very readability of what should essentially look like a three-column table with telegraphic entries.

I give an example.

December 20 is the scheduled entrance of Mars in Paola's natal Third House. On the 15th of December they steal Paola's car; or she bumps into a car; or she loses her phone; perhaps her line remains isolated and she cannot receive or send calls and fax (by the way, at the time of this writing my phone line was disconnected seven day ago, and the telephone company says that my tribute to Mars in the 3rd House is not enough). Then Paola, next to the date of the 20th December, in the right column would simply write -5, which means 'the entrance presumably took place five days ahead of schedule.'

The entrance of Mars in the Fourth House radix is scheduled on the 14th of February. She would write on the line below, *Mars in 4th, expected on Feb. 14th*. The 10th of February Paola is called with urgency because her father had a heart attack, or perhaps she would have an unexpected trouble at home and she would have to call for carpenters or builders. She will consequently score in the right column, -4. And so on.

At the end, the astrologer will read a single table with about eighteen to twenty lines at most. If the data is fairly constant, as it should be, especially if those who draw up the table are keen observers of the facts of their life and follow the advice of a book as in my *Transits and Solar Returns*, they should produce a fairly clear log of events that help you correct their time of birth forward or backward by some minutes, until you are able to get an almost exact time of birth.

This is a method that I have been following for many years – I can say that it works perfectly. Do not chase mythologies of astrologers who claim, "I'll tell you even the second you were born!" You will see that this 'toy' is very efficient and it will help you a lot!

5.
Transits of Mars

The transits of Mars, speaking from a point of view of time, are something exactly between the so–called fast transits and the slow transits. In fact Mars, seen from the Earth, takes about two years to complete a tour around the Zodiac. It therefore remains in each sign less than two months, although sometimes it so happens that it prolongs its stay in a sign. In other words, some sign may be 'forced' to host it for more than two months. Ancient called it the 'lesser malefic' to distinguish it from Saturn, which was the 'greater malefic'.

In fact we must admit that Mars plays a role wherever there is a disgrace in our earthly life, although nowadays it is not politically correct to speak of anything in negative terms, and somebody clutches at straws trying to find out something good even in the worst events. Similar to the fever that accompanies any disease, Mars also accompanies other more important transits marking our miseries. Not only Mars seldom acts alone – or if it does, it only causes lesser damage – together with slower transits, it might provoke much harm.

It is my opinion that a passage of Mars, as well as those of Saturn, can help an astrologer rectify (i.e., correct) the hour of birth of a native. In fact the entrance of Mars in a House is rather visible for the immediate damage it causes; thus one can establish – together with other elements – where the cusps of a House stands, with a reliable approximation. It has to be said that in my opinion Mars is the second significator of one's libido after the Sun. The position of the Sun in a natal House generally shows the native's mental direction, i.e. whether he/she is a card player, a Lovelace, an indefatigable worker… Immediately after comes Mars: from its position in the Houses you can also tell whether the native is a valetudinarian, a passionate reader, a stickler for friendship… Thus when either Mars or the Sun enter each House, they tell you where you focus you energy on to.

For example, the passage of Mars into the 4th House doesn't only indicate trouble in your environment, but also your commitment to repair, restore, and renovate it; or to get a loan etc. I can then claim without any exaggeration that the transit of the ruler of Aries and Scorpio considered either in its liaisons with other celestials or in each of the twelve Houses, comes with both positive and negative valence.

Transit Mars in the First House

When Mars goes through your 1st House you feel you have a greater charge of energy. It is not merely physical energy: your mind is also determined and clear as never. You would then take fair, brave and sharp decisions. Those who are usually accustomed to such behaviour wouldn't really perceive the beauty of this transit; but those whose disposition is not prone to immediate decisions would feel gratified by such a wave of determination and willpower. They would feel the thrill of taking decisions without any dithering and second thoughts. The goals would be clear in your mind, and you would reach them overcoming all hindrances or delays. You would show more backbone when making significant choices.

You would behave like a leader, tending to give direct orders to your collaborators, yet without being authoritarian. Those around you would perceive your determination of these days, and would appreciate the clarity of your actions. This Mars 'on your skin' would make you more sincere and direct; less diplomatic; more determined to achieve your programmed goals. You would like to leave practically in the present, rather than in the past or in the future. According to the ancient Latin motto *carpe diem*, you would pluck the day, seize the chance, and you would be prompt to react in real time. You would be able to assert your rights with your employers or senior managers; you would be able to have frank discussions with the authorities, without staying in awe of them any longer. You would also be able to manage better your familial issues, where you'd prove to be resolute without being tyrannical. This transit would give you a moment of true inner strength, not a mere show of appearance.

This strength would find an expression also at the physical level of course: so be prepared for a huge amount of work. Seize the chance then, for if you have a backlog of work or if you are late with something, under this transit you would be able to get through much work, either physical or mental. Your enhanced psychophysical energy would lead you to engage in sports. If you usually practice sports, you would go in for a sport more often, or with more enthusiasm than usual. Any discipline would do: football, tennis, volleyball, ping–pong… It is a very good period to join a fitness club, or to start playing a sport at a competitive level, or simply on a regular basis. For those who aren't really keen sportsmen (or sportswomen) interminable walks or jogging in the park or on the beach would also do. Less lively people might simply go trekking to the heights, or gathering mushrooms in the most appropriate sites.

For sure this transit would increase your sexual activity – this refers especially to men. If the transit takes place with dissonant angles compared with the rest of the natal chart, or simultaneously with other disharmonic transits, then you had better take control over your temper, for your overbearing manner would also increase. You would be particularly prone to arguments and you run the risk of spoiling some important relationship for your temporary restiveness. You would tend to trample on the feelings of those around you, and to impose yourself on others like a little tyrant. You would be quite intolerant towards others' needs, and you would argue for trivial reasons. You run a serious risk of wounding yourself handling sharp tools or being involved in a nose–to–tail crash.

It is a rather dangerous time in fact for driving cars or riding motorbikes; climbing mountains, stairs or ladders; and for any other activity normally considered as dangerous, such as lighting fires with gasoline, handling guns, diving from the reef, or playing any risky sport. You had better channel this excess of energy to more frequent sexual activity. During this transit people are likely to go to the dentist or to undergo a minor surgery. Do not worry: perhaps you would simply be ill with a slight flu.

Transit Mars in the Second House

When Mars enters the 2nd House of your birth chart your energies are fully projected towards increasing your income. You think about your own survival more than usual, committing yourself to take more profit from your environment. If you have entrepreneurial skills you would be able to make good use of them during this transit – not necessarily for long–term projects or for decisive professional changes. In fact this transit might simply announce an interlude in which you may happen to have an inspiration about increasing your income, perhaps selling things that you don't use any more. You would therefore follow with increased attentions the classified advertisements, and/ or you would resolve to put an ad yourself. You might make good deals visiting websites of auctions on the Internet. Even if your usual work is not of a materialist kind, during this transit you would redirect it towards greed, trying to pocket as much money you can.

You might make your mind up to get a credit card (perhaps *another* credit card); to apply for a loan; or to ask a friend for money – in fact you would feel certain that you would be able to give the money back. It is also a good time to open a shop, to start on a new business (of any kind), to become an agent, to open a new workshop and so on. At the same time you would feel the need to care for your own looks more than usual. For example you might resolve to start on a slimming diet or to shave or to change your hairstyle. Often people slightly change their way of dressing during this transit. In other cases you would deal with the notion of image linked to the theatre, the cinema, photography, computer–aided–design and so on. In this case you would like to act as an amateur, or to buy a camera or a video camera or a video recorder, and work with pictures – either your own pictures, or others'. This transit might announce the birth of a real passion on this subject. It is also a favourable moment to learn how to use a new graphical software utility, or to buy a new television set or a new monitor for your computer. If the transit happens with dissonant angles or together with other disharmonic transits, then you had better try to avoid expenses; otherwise you would run the risk of a little drain of money.

You would tend to spend much on unimportant things. You might also lose money because you lend them without asking for securities, or because you invest them in the stock market. During this transit your money might even be stolen. So beware of thieves, robbers, burglars. Somebody might pay you with uncovered cheques, or you might be a victim of a fraud. Due to the symbols associated with the Red planet, you can be expected to spend money on motors, mechanical tools, weapons… Wounds or cuts might spoil your appearance. Interventions of cosmetic surgery are also possible.

Transit Mars in the Third House

With Mars transiting in your 3rd House radix you would direct the utmost of your psychophysical energies towards communication in the broadest meaning of the term. You would wish to get in touch with people more than usual. You would realize that your thoughts are more penetrating and centrifugal during this transit. Your mind would focus onto the outer world, gaining in lucidity and clarity at the same time. You would be able to expose logical, direct, consistent, straightforward, clever, smart and sharp considerations.

Your capacity of speech would increase as well. You would use a greater number of terms, since you would happen to use rarely used verbs and substantives that you thought you had forgotten. You would spend more time on the telephone; you would make more calls and you would answer more calls. The subjects of these calls might be delicate or demanding. Perhaps the persons you would speak with would be important or demanding. You would also write more, perhaps several hours a day, e.g. to send a newsletter or invitation cards. Your determination and will power would be easily channelled in phone conversations and text messages. You would also like to navigate on the Web, spending much of your time on it. You would like to travel, and you might resolve to drive for hours, or to ride your motorbike for miles. During these days you would find a special pleasure in driving. You would find it relaxing, especially on the motorways. You would spend more energy than usual for a brother, a cousin, a brother–in–law, or for a younger male friend. For example you might decide to go and visit them. You might also happen to perform some task concerning communication, such as mounting a satellite dish on your roof at home, or installing an interphone line at your work place.

Your enhanced mental clarity would help you study with increased proficiency, attending courses or giving lessons, taking part in seminars and conferences, passing exams and so on. You would be in a special mood for reading, studying, and writing. You might then make an important report, prepare a speech, complete a chapter of a book, or simply keep a log. If this transit comes together with disharmonic aspects or with other bad transits, then it might be quite risky with regard to road accidents. Be careful with whatever you do on the road: drive a car, ride a motorbike, cross the street or get into a bus.

You would easily argue with the clerks beyond the windows, with the shop assistants, or with the policemen on the street. You might have some argument also with a brother, a cousin, a brother–in–law or a younger friend. You might also get bad news concerning the aforementioned persons. You might receive unpleasant or menacing letters or phone calls. Your tools of communication might break down: e.g. your mobile phone, your cordless phone, your modem, the fax machine, the printer, and so on. The press might deal with you and you might appear in the papers, but it would not be for good news. You might have an argument with your publisher. You might have troubles during journeys, e.g. due to strikes, missed or delayed trains, blocked airports, failures of your car and so on. You might run the risk of smoking excessively.

Transit Mars in the Fourth House

With Mars transiting in your birth 4th House you spend much energy on your habitat, i.e. not only the place you live in, but also the place you work in. In other words, you would spend more time than usual dealing with the four walls 'containing' you. You would plan to move, or to buy an estate. You would apply for a loan to purchase an estate or a time–share house. Perhaps you would go with your partner and visit houses to rent or to buy. You might also go and see a house or book a room at a hotel for your next holidays. More likely, you would decide on restoration at home or at the workplace, for example a shop or a workshop, etc. You would like to do it yourself, perhaps you would be able to paint a room or to fit a carpet, as well as many other little or significant tasks that usually belong in the realm of skilled labour. Dealing with your home would be a pleasure. Perhaps you would simply project to remove or to replace a piece of furniture one of these days, or have a new kitchen designed especially for you, but you might also resolve to make concrete steps and make shopping in an interior design store.

This transit might also correspond to a period of routine maintenance at home, such as cleaning the windows, having the curtains washed, tidying up your bookshelves, and so on. You would deal more with your parents too: you would go and visit them, or they would stay at your place for a while; you would take them here and there, dealing with their bureaucratic issues and so on. If this transit takes place with disharmonic angles or simultaneously with other negative passages, you could expect possible damages at home. It might be the spreading of a small fire, electrical household appliances going wrong, windows shattering, porcelain objects smashing into pieces, etc.

You would probably receive bad news concerning your habitat, such as letters of your lessee giving notice to quit (if you are a tenant), or letters of your tenant claiming the reimbursement of certain expenses (if you are a lessee), or a notice regarding unexpected shared running expenses, etc. In other words: bad news concerning real estate. It might also happen that you realize that you cannot easily pay back your loan, or that a restoration comes with much higher expenses than you had expected or planned. If you own a trailer or a van, you might have an accident with them. Your parents undergo surgery or become ill, or you argue with them. For a few days you might be hospitalized yourself. The hard disk of your computer, or any other magnetic support, becomes unserviceable. Those who suffer from troubles in the stomach might face a worsening of their conditions.

Transit Mars in the Fifth House

When Mars transits into your radix 5th house your libido is directed towards everything that can be considered as a play, a game, a recreation. Your most impellent desire is to have fun, to be happy, not to think of anything, and to enjoy as much as you can. You would leave worries and neglect things you have to do, for you would consider that duty can wait. What you wish to do now is to have a break and go for a holiday. It is a good span of time to go on a journey, to spend a week–end alone looking for adventure, or with your beloved one.

You might as well remain where you live, but if so you would go out more often at night, e.g. to the cinema, to the theatre, to concerts, to the restaurant, to the disco, to the night club, to the casino and so on... You might discover or rediscover the pleasure of spending nights at home, playing bridge, poker, bingo or any other indoor game with your friends. If you are a musician, you would play more often for delight, with your friends; and if you are a sportsperson, this time you would practice your sport for pure delight. The bottom line is not *what* you do, but *how* you do it. For example, if you like to read, and you usually read essays or studies or reports concerning your job, with this transit you would allow yourself a moment's rest by reading science fiction or a thriller or a love story.

For sure your sexual life would also reflect this situation: this transit would give you a season of very intense satisfactions. It is also a very good period to procreate or to plan to have a child: this refers both to male and female natives. Sometimes people speculate with stocks during this transit, because dealing with the stock market may be a profession, but it is basically also a game. You might also take part in a quiz game: there are so many of them nowadays. If you are an artist, you would become more creative than ever. If you are a teacher, you would spend more energy on didactics. If the transit takes place with dissonant angles with other celestials, or if it comes together with other disharmonic transits, then you might perform a sequel of exaggerations due to your excess of sensual libido.

In other words, you would run the risk to exaggerate for your eagerness to satisfy your body. Thus you might be involved in little accidents because of your hunger for having fun, e.g. you might end up playing dangerous sports, or driving the car after having spent a night at the disco smoking and drinking much.

The excess of sensuality and of sexual activity might lead you to provoke undesired pregnancies, and/or to contract a sexual disease. Your relationship with your sons and/or daughters might become worse during this transit, provoking arguments and tension. One of your kids might become ill or be a victim of an accident; they might simply face a lesser affliction such as failing an exam, losing a match, breaking with a friend, and so on…

Transit Mars in the Sixth House

When Mars enters your natal 6th House your energies focus onto your own body, leading you to have a better care for it from the point of view of health or of beauty. You would resolve to feel better, to do more for yourself, and to take better care of your own psychophysical health. It is the right moment to join a fitness club, or to go in for sport at home or in a club. You might resolve to buy a rowing machine or an exercise bicycle.

You might start on slimming or detoxifying diet. A good way to purify your body would be to avoid, for the time being, eating meat, drinking alcohol, or introducing sugar into your organism. Your willpower would become stronger when dealing with these matters, so you could seize the chance and quit smoking or any other detoxifying factor, perhaps also certain useless pills that you take without medical prescription. During this passage you would follow the Latin motto *mens sana in corpore sano* as strictly as possible.

Do physical activities, sweat, take saunas, have healthy warm showers, undergo mud therapies and whatever may be useful and healthy for your skin, your face, your hair… If you suffer from arthrosis or from rheumatism, this is a good period for remedial gymnastics, Shiatsu, acupuncture, pranic–therapy… You would even be able to perform these activities for others, because the energy that resides in you during this transit may refer to the care of your own body, as well as to the care of others' body. So you might learn how to practice massages or subscribe to courses on chiropractic, macrobiotic, rehabilitating physiotherapy, and so on. The same refers to beauty treatment such as suntan lamps or electro depilation: you might receive such therapies, or render them to others. You might as well resolve to live in seclusion in beauty farms where you can take long walks in the woods besides other treatments. Mars in the 6th House might also direct your energies towards work: in this case you can seize the chance and get through a good deal of work. You would become a sort of workaholic, and you would be able to spend hours working without pause.

This transit favours any sort of manual activity and do–it–yourself such as lathing, knitting, drilling, kneading, and so on. If this passage takes place over dissonant angles with other celestials, or if it comes together with other bad transits, you may stand fair chances to become ill; in the worst event you might even have to undergo surgery. But in the majority of cases it's simply a matter of dental care. Also fever and infections are possible. You may be damaged by therapies applied without due care: for example you might faint due to a pressure drop under a mud application; or you might have a bone broken due to an awkward chiropractic massage; or you might be intoxicated by a wrong diet or a wrong medicine, and so on. You might also have arguments at work, with senior managers and colleagues. Accidents at work are also possible. You might argue with a collaborator. You might have to dismiss a servant. One of your servants might get wounded or ill. This transit may also announce the wounding or death of a pet.

Transit Mars in the Seventh House

When Mars is in transit in your natal 7th House you spend virtually all of your energy for being in contact with others. Regardless of whether you are an introvert or an extrovert; an egotist or someone who's sincerely willing to melt your own Ego with others; under this transit you would do your utmost to converge towards your neighbour, i.e. a single partner or a society, a group, a coalition, a gang, a club... Rather than just willing, since we are under the realm of the active Mars, you would make concrete steps in order to construct such a situation in which you might eventually refer to yourself not as *I*, but as *we*. You would declare your feeling to somebody in order to start a relationship, cohabitation, marriage. Your eagerness for relationships would find practical and factual ways to express itself. If you have already a steady partner, you would probably fix the date for your marriage or for the beginning of your cohabitation. If you have already fixed up the date, you would deal actively with all the administrative issues in order to make your marriage or cohabitation possible.

For example you would chose the town hall or the temple for the celebration; you would book the restaurant; have the invitations printed; arrange for the decorations at the florist, and so on. To make a long story short, you would roll up your sleeves and do something real for this sort of projects. During these days you might be overwhelmed by practical duties concerning the organization of a ceremony which is not merely a ceremony, but the beginning of a real story with a steady partner with whom you'd share your life. You would feel strongly motivated and nobody, nothing would be able to stop you.

If on the contrary, you are already and happily married, and you have to establish a society (be it a business enterprise, a study, a political commitment), well in this case you would act differently, yet with the same spirit; that is to say, unite with others. This transit convinces you that the only way for you to grow is to share your path with one or more persons. If it weren't for this periodical transit, only the three signs of Air would possibly match, while all the rest would probably keep on their own. Evidently nature (or perhaps the Zodiac, if you prefer) has organized things differently, and makes you be alternatively and periodically sociable and unsociable just enough to balance the strengths of life avoiding any exaggeration from one side or another.

Since this is the transit of sociability, you would join a political party; a philosophical or religious coalition; a club; a cooperative; a brotherhood of any kind. Even if you generally don't like politics, for the first time in your life you might get the chance to deal with politics in the noblest meaning of the term, under this transit. You would surely spend much energy for your partner, who would face quite hectic days. Perhaps he/she would be able to have his/her rights recognized during this transit. You would also be attracted by uniforms and by martial roles. But if the transit takes place with disharmonic aspects or together with other dissonant transits, then you have to expect a good amount of stamped paper (i.e. bureaucracy) for you or for your partner.

More generally, you would face many battles, struggles, wars, regardless of whether you cause them, or you simply have to defend yourself from others' attacks. More frequently it would be quarrels with your partner, but it may also happen that you would have to face serious conflicts involving (or not involving) stamped paper, judges, lawyers, and tribunals. Perhaps you wouldn't be involved directly and personally: maybe you would simply have to assist arguments. Maybe law would deal with you, which is seldom a pleasant thing. In the worst case you might be visited by the Police, Customs and Excise officers and so on. It might be just a routine check, or something more serious. If other important transits let you foresee it, you might even be a victim of an act of terrorism, robbery, menaces, mugging or damages to your goods. You might simply experience troubles with the peripheral devices of your computer, or with the cable or wireless connection between the computer and its devices.

Transit Mars in the Eighth House

With Mars transiting in the 8th House of their natal chart many people ask for loans or deal with bureaucracy in order to apply for a credit line. You too would move towards increasing your finance through legacies, endowments, pensions, severance pay, donations and so on. This would prevail over all other activities of yours. Whatever you do in this field during this transit would succeed. You would aim to earn more, and you would probably get positive results. You would be able to employ your best energies and to act with unusual pragmatism for the sake of converting your efforts into money. During this period you would easily have something to do with notaries, lawyers, bank managers, directors of financial houses. At a lower level, you would probably show interest for sex.

Also in this case, you would act factually in this field, dealing with sex much more than usual. Rather than a sensual call, this transit causes a strong erotic stimulation, i.e. you would consider sex mainly at a cerebral level. You might therefore wish to unchain your sexual fantasies and ask for your partner's collaboration in discovering new ways of having sex. It is also possible that you would spend energy on things or activities concerning the symbolism of death. For example you might succeed in saving a dear person from death; or you might simply plan to rehabilitate your family's tomb.

Your increased interest in death would lead you to take part in séances, contact mediums, and make researches in esoteric or occult subjects. If the transit takes place with dissonant angles with several elements of your birth chart, or together with other dissonant transits, it is possible that you would face many difficulties, especially legal ones, concerning the devise of a legacy, the distribution of goods between you and your partner, or between you and your next of kin. Usually in these cases the parties concerned charge a lawyer to deal with the matter. You might also experience troubles dealing with liquidation; perhaps you would find it hard to be granted a pension. You would have to struggle to be granted a loan, and it would be probably refused to you. You might have difficulties in refunding a loan. You might have to pay unexpected taxes. You would realize that your current account is overdrawn. You might have to repay a sum that you do not own currently.

You might have to pay according to a timetable but you would have run out of money. If you had obtained money from usurers, during this transit they might intimidate you to seek their money back with interests. You might argue with your partner concerning your common goods. He or she might be in financial troubles, causing you a significant loss of money. At a sexual level, you would feel an increased impulse that you aren't able to satisfy or that you satisfy in an unorthodox way. You might then have unpleasant meetings looking for sex. You might have sex with criminals. You would run the risk of getting sexual diseases.

You would be stricken by death. e.g. the death of a relative. In the worst events a possible interpretation of this transit (provided that other transits confirm so) may be that your life is in danger. You might have awful experiences during a séance or dealing with esoteric subjects. The burying of a relative, or the relocation of his/her body, might give you trouble. Your family's tomb might be damaged. You might have to spend on the burial of a next of kin.

Transit Mars in the Ninth House

You spend much energy in search of whatever is *far away*, when Mars passes through your 9th House; *far away* to be intended both in the geographical (another land) and in the metaphysical–transcendent meaning of the term. Your usual desire of travelling somewhere is increased by this transit. It is rare that people don't travel during this transit. For sure you would move too: if not abroad, you would go to another town at least. Still, you would stand fair chances to go abroad, although it might be for a few days only. It is a good moment to deal with foreign subjects. This transit favours learning languages.

This refers also to programming languages for computers. You would spend much energy to establish or to develop connections with far–off people or sites, e.g. you might wish to have a broadband Internet connection installed. In any case you would surely spend much time on the Internet, browsing the World Wide Web. You would also spend much time dealing with your car or with your motorbike. Not only would your interest in philosophy, theology, yoga, astrology, Eastern culture etc. increase in theory: you would also take concrete steps in these fields. For example you would buy books on these subjects; you would study; attend courses, congresses and conferences on these themes; you would learn techniques and methods; you would contact masters, and so on. You would correspond with people in far–away countries. If you are a university student, you would commence studying important subjects. You might take a man of your environment abroad, perhaps for medical reasons. At the same time you would be spurred to engage in sports, and if you already do it, you would practise sports more than usual. You might show a particular interest towards animality. If the transit happens in a disharmonic context, it might even announce a road accident.

Therefore be careful when driving or while crossing the street. You might also stumble and fall when boarding or getting off a bus, or any other vehicle. Sometimes the accident is not strictly related with vehicles: with this transit some people may have accidents simply walking from one room to another. Your car may break down. You may receive bad news from abroad (or from far away). One of your next of kin may experience an unpleasant event abroad, or perhaps he/she may have to travel to undergo surgery. You might argue for ideological reasons. You might have to struggle with uncertain results for matters of principle, perhaps concerning your deepest convictions. You might have a clash with opponents from other towns, or during a journey. Under such a negative transit, you had better avoid moving at all. Also take good care when you are involved in sports, especially the ones commonly considered as risky or dangerous sports.

For students at university this transit usually means a period of particular work pressure. For everybody, it also means a period of struggle for defending or asserting your thoughts. You might also be wounded by an animal. Your modem or your mobile phone might go wrong.

Transit Mars in the Tenth House

When Mars transits in the 10th House of your natal chart you aim high, very high. Rather than simply aspiring to achieve better result concerning your professional status or your social condition, during this transit you would take factual steps to achieve your goals. You would spend much energy for your own emancipation, in the broadest meaning of this term. During this transit teenagers may obtain a higher degree of independence from their parents, e.g. being allowed to come home late at night. Married people may emancipate talking up to their partner. This transit would surely help you to get rid of any sort of bonds thanks to your own willpower and your determination, enhanced by this transit. Such a psychophysical charge might help you stop smoking, drinking alcohol, taking unnecessary pills. Most people under deep psychological analysis, under this transit become able to quit their psychoanalytic therapy. The fixedness of your intents, the clear vision of what you really want, gives you a special strength that allows you to go steadfastly towards your own professional or social growth. It is therefore a good moment to apply for an advance, i.e. to obtain a better contract at work, or to get a post involving higher responsibilities inside your company. During this transit it is likely that you succeed in setting up a business overcoming possible fear that may have prevented you from establishing an independent enterprise so far. Several business or industrial enterprises were born under this transit.

During this passage your political ambition may also grow significantly. Your emancipation may also arrive from learning to swim or to use the computer, or from conquering your own fear of flying. You would spend much energy on your mother; perhaps your mother would experience a period of great vitality and activity. Nonetheless, if the transit takes place together with other dissonant transits, it might announce a hard time of struggles with uncertain results, connected with your wish to obtain a better job or more favourable job conditions a work. You might be violently questioned. You might be attacked by new and old enemies. Your work might become endangered; perhaps you are supposed to face directly certain specific problems that have prevented you from growing so far. You might have to struggle harshly to establish a better place under the sun. You might be in contrast with your mother. Your mother might be ill, perhaps she needs surgery. Accidents at work are also possible.

Transit Mars in the Eleventh House

When Mars transits over your birth 11th House you do your utmost in order to help your friends, even if you are not usually keen on company. You would have a stronger feeling of friendship and solidarity for those around you. You would factually do something for a friend and you would tend to behave with a stronger sense of comradeship.

You would have more social life and you would avoid staying home on your own. You would have more occasions of meeting people and making new friends. Regardless of your efforts you would realize that chances of meeting people would naturally multiply under this transit. At the same time your friends would offer you their helping hand, and you would understand how important friends can be. You had better go and ask for assistance and sponsors during this transit. If you ask correctly, without pretending, you would be granted what you need. If during this transit you looked for those people in high places whom you had met some time ago, he/she would surely help you solve a problem. This transit leads people to make many projects in any field of their life: e.g. refurbishing a house or founding an enterprise.

You might also spend much energy trying to avoid a death, or to have it postponed as much as possible. If this transit happens with disharmonic angles, or if it takes places together with other negative transits, then you would have to expect the end of a friendship. You would become rather aggressive with friends, and your friends would also show aggressiveness towards you. A friend of yours might do something wrong, or become ill, or have an accident. Persons in high places might treat you badly. You might meet many hindrances to have your projects accomplished. You might also make destructive plans. A male close to you (such as your husband, boyfriend, brother, or a male friend) might quarrel with his friends. He might also fraternize with people who later on would prove to be criminals or socially dangerous persons. In the worst cases such a negative transit might announce the death of a friend or relative. If other transits confirm so, your own life might be in danger.

Transit Mars in the Twelfth House

With Mars transiting in your natal 12th House you would spend much energy in research. If you are a professional researcher, this would be an excellent period for your work. If you operate in other fields, during these days you would feel the need for a deeper endopsychical research. You might therefore start writing a log, perhaps your memories. This transit favours readings and studies especially of esoteric, astrological, psychological and theological subjects, just to mention a few. If you are a practicing believer you might seize the chance and pray much, perhaps go into retreat, staying in touch with the most sacred things you believe in. Otherwise you might attend congresses and conferences of astrology, psychology, philosophy and so on.

It is a perfect time for psychoanalysis. Everybody has in them to some degree to offer nursing assistance to others. Whatever may be the degree of this tendency, during this transit your wish of assisting people would grow significantly, leading you to factual acts of solidarity: e.g. you might simply contribute to organizations such as Caritas, the Red Cross, UNICEF and so on; you might also resolve to volunteer in one of these organizations. If you usually act in your private sphere rather than in society, you would help your dear ones. If you take psychotropic drugs, this transit would strengthen your will against them and you might even quit taking them. The same refers to drug addiction, if you are facing such a situation of suffering.

During this transit your political or ideological struggles would become stronger and more concrete. Your battles would be more vivid and efficient, especially if you are struggling to claim your own rights. You would also fight successfully against your hidden enemies. Yet, if this passage takes place with disharmonic angles or simultaneously with other very dissonant transits, then it is a quite negative, if not dangerous, astrological factor. It might announce bad experiences concerning your religious or philosophical credo; harmful consequences of a meeting with a self–proclaimed magician or astrologer. You might also have an argument with a psychologist or with a priest.

You might be mugged by a drug addict. You or someone close to you may have to undergo surgery. You might have to be hospitalized. You might be jailed or confined in the widest meaning of the term, e.g. you might have to pass quarantine. In the worst cases, if other elements of your birth chart confirm so, you might actually have to go to jail. Secret enemies might act against you during this transit. People might spread canard and slander against you. You or your closest relatives might live a period of bad popularity. Road accidents are also possible. You might experience mishaps in any field of your existence: health, love, marriage, work, finance, family, friends… This transit, if negative, might also announce possible bereavement.

6.
The interrogation

This operation requires great practical experience and many tricks of the trade – in the best sense of the term of course – as well as a vast knowledge of astrology as a whole, of psychology, of elements of physiognomy, of medicine and of many other disciplines in addition.

For example, knowing that an individual with protruding eyeballs almost certainly suffers (or could suffer over time), from serious problems of the thyroid, is a piece of information that goes beyond the narrow astrological context, but it could serve well during the interview with your counselee. Let us make it clear: you should be face to face with your counselee, for this questioning can not be replaced with a telephone consultation even if you have the native's photo in front of you.

This is because as an astrologer, you should not miss a single detail of the individual sitting in front of you, from the very moment of his arrival to the moment of his going out of the door of your place. Everything is extremely important – no detail should be neglected.

Note the following: Does Mr. Smith arrive on time? Or is he early? Perhaps, he is late. How does he behave, how does he justify his being very late or very early? What kind of stance does he adopt? How does he gesticulate? How much time does it take for him to answer your questions? Does he tend to withdraw? Does he open up instead? Is he talkative or does he tend to be silent? Does he try to seduce those with whom he talks, or does he show indifference? Does he wriggle about? Is he able to keep still for many minutes? Does he need to smoke? Does he ask to drink, to go to the bathroom, to make a phone call? How does he behave when you point out contradictions in his answers? Is his attitude accommodating or biting? Is he a careful listener or does he show a good amount of superficiality? Does he show evident signs of pathologies? Is his breath so heavy that it might suggest liver problems? How does he care for his nails? Has he grown such a belly that may indicate his state of satisfaction with life? Is he tightened or relaxed?

We could go on for hours. To make a long story short, in my opinion this is when the good astrologer demonstrates that he is different from the others. From their ability of asking questions, one can recognize those astrologers who have decades of experience, accrued not for meeting three or four people each month, but on a very large number of counselees. This is why I agree with my venerable master André Barbault, who claimed that a great astrologer must have practised a lot. Without practice, one may even become a good student of astrology, not an astrologer.

Let us stick to the interview. A good homeopathic doctor always starts his diagnosis with a long and highly detailed questioning. My baptism with homeopathy will remain an indelible memory in me. I was twenty years old. I went to Rome to request the great professor Antonio Negro prescribe medication for me. In his study, in the gloom of the room, we sat at his desk facing each other: the professor asked a lot of questions and as I answered he noted then down on a big book. The questioning went on for over ninety minutes, while the exercise of prescription itself lasted only a few minutes. In fact, he had received the right information directly from my mouth – the physical examination on my body only served to confirm what he had already understood. The homeopathic doctor would ask questions like, "Are you always cold? or always warm?"

OK, let us pause here for a moment. You would answer with a *yes* or *no*, and if the doctor is not a good one, he would simply note your answer. On the contrary, if he is a valued researcher and professional, he would never accept your answer as good, but he would make many counter–questions to verify it. For example he may ask, "When in bed, do you look for a warm place for you feet, or for a cool place? Do you usually keep your shirt neck open (unbuttoned) or closed (buttoned)? In winter do you tend to keep the window slightly open? Or perhaps do you usually sit next to a radiator?" He would keep on until, after many counter–questions, he would be able to write down, without any doubt, a single word written in capital letters: COLD or WARM.

The same must be done during the astrological examination with the aim of verifying the time of birth of a native. The main direction that must guide you is the identification of the native's *libido* – which, I repeat once again, is primarily indicated by the position of the Sun in the Houses of his birth chart, and only secondarily, by the position of Mars or of a stellium in the Houses of his birth chart. Let's just look at a practical example. Once a teacher of high school came to me for counselling and we had quite a long conversation. Eventually he asked, "How come you haven't told me anything about my children?" "Because in your birth chart they do occupy a tiny space, sir." "But they are my whole life!" "OK, we'll see." Then I asked him how many hours of the day he usually spends with his children. He replied that he does not see them at all – he goes out early in the morning while the kids are just getting up. Returning home, he literally locks himself (turning the key) in his study, listening to classical music and reading or studying.

Around 17 he usually goes out to meet his partner; he would come home late at night when the kids are already asleep. Would *you* say that this gentleman's sons are *his whole life*? Thus it becomes clear that is not enough to put your hand on your heart and say that you are strongly burning from passion for someone or something. For it's the facts that tell you exactly *where your libido goes*. Giacomo Casanova could genuinely claim that his predominantly sexual *libido* was true *lust*, in the facts and not only in aspirations, because when he saw a woman – beautiful or ugly or fat or young or old or crippled – he could not stop thinking of 'raping' her.

His energy was so strongly spurring him in this direction that he would usually succeed in having an intercourse – exactly because for him this was 'a bee in his bonnet'. The same goes for those food lovers who are starting to plan their day thinking about everything they would eat throughout the day, or those athletes who get up in the morning with a single purpose: run a few kilometres more than the previous day. Here is where you should start from. You should also start from the most striking signs that, in the native's birth chart, may indicate possible major tragedies or great joys of life.

I remember a man of about sixty years. He came to me and swore that he was born on the twelfth stroke of noon, and so on... (You know, the usual story that I have already told you). Well in the middle of his Seventh House I noticed the dreadful conjunction Mars–Saturn, almost perfect to the degree. I immediately thought of verifying whether this conjunction could be in the Eighth House rather than in the Seventh, so I asked, "Is there in your life a very dramatic death, which has left a terrible mark in your life?" He answered, "Yes, it's the tragedy of my life. My 20 year–old son died, no one knows if he was killed or he committed suicide, and one month later the boy's alleged murderer killed himself." Then I said, "If so, you can not be born even a minute after 10:45. Please ask your register of births to produce an extract of your full birth record. Then come back to me." It turned out that he was born around ten o'clock in the morning.

As I said before, the first thing that must guide you should be detecting the position of the Sun in the native's Houses of birth. Please refer to the relevant section of this volume. If you are lucky, you can unmask a false time in ten minutes. Of course you can not certainly say at what time the person was really born. But you can exclude with certainty that he was *not* born after a certain time or before another time, and if you are able to delimit the native's time of birth at least from the one side, this is already a huge advantage. As I mentioned earlier, almost all the recorded times of birth are rounded up.

So if already during the interrogation you can obtain evidence that the subject was born, say, 45 minutes before the recorded time, this is quite an important result because it prevents you from wasting much time and producing mistaken astrological readings in the coming years. In this respect, the ideal scenario is when the Sun of the native is, say, in the Third House, six or seven degrees away from the Imum Coeli (or in the 6th House at the same distance from the Descendant or in the 9th House at the same distance from MC, and so on...). If so, you can immediately establish a fundamental fact, namely whether the rounding up of the time of birth is limited within a frame of 15 to 30 minutes or whether it is rounded up of more than half an hour. This is already a great advantage that can totally change the perspective from which you would look at a birth chart.

Remember though, that particular positions of the celestials (like the aforementioned conjunction of Mars and Saturn) may be as useful as the Sun in the Houses, because they usually represent extraordinary events in the life of a person that can not go unnoticed.

In proceeding with such an analysis, you must take into account the age of the native. If he or she is eighteen years old, probably the already mentioned conjunction of Mars and Saturn will only show all of its power when your counselee is thirty years older. Conversely, if you are analyzing the astrological situation of a person of 50–60 years, things are different because in the overwhelming majority of cases, at that age that conjunction has already manifested itself clearly.

In this regard I have collected a small set of rather disturbing cases of people born on the same day, thus having that very same strict conjunction between the 'little malefic' and the 'great malefic' celestials. Three cases follow having the mentioned conjunction in their natal 7th House. Case A. A lady belonging to high society is arrested. She spends twenty days in a women's prison because a terrorist's organizer contained her phone number. It was a mistake of course: as soon as a judge questions her, facts come to the fore, and the woman is freed – yet this is the worst experience of her life. Case B. A man from Sardinia is kidnapped by mistake and held captive for two months in the caves of Barbagia, the mountain area of inner Sardinia. Case C. The sister of a lady born with that conjunction is murdered. In the relevant trial, the lady assists helplessly to the murderers' acquittal.

In the Eighth House, this conjunction brings countless cases of failures, bankruptcy, economic reversals, husbands squandering a fortune at stake, precipitating financial situations. In 99% of cases of this conjunction lying in the natal Ninth House, I have found events relating to serious traffic accidents. Still, as usual, the counselees may deny with all their might, in good faith, that they have never suffered from anything. I remember a lady who swore that there had been no major accident ever in her family. She also denied that any close relative had ever had an accident either. When it turned out that she had fallen very badly stumbling on a sidewalk, almost breaking half of the bones of her body, thus suffering from serious and permanent injuries, she said that she thought that when I say, 'accident' I was referring only to cars ramming into each other or knocking down a person. That is why, I repeat yet another time, for each answer you receive from the native you have to take at least ten counter–questions, trying to figure out where the native's possible psychological repression is, if any, be it voluntary or involuntary.

One day I was interviewing a retired lady born with an ugly Saturn in her 9th House. To my questions on its possible consequences she replied, "Nothing, nothing ever happened to me. I don't remember anything disagreeable happening abroad or with foreigners." I plied her with my usual ten or maybe twenty counter–questions, but I got nowhere. So we started probing other subjects, when the lady had a sort of flash and exclaimed, "May it be the fact that at the age of twenty I married a Swede who left me the very next day and did not ever turn up since then?"

So you see: doubt, always doubt; distrust even your own mother and yourself. Investigating the psychological mechanisms of lies and repression is not the scope of this volume. The only thing you have to remember is that, regardless of the cause which determines them, lies usually are a good portion of the speech of counselees. As an astrologer, you have to become a skilled Sherlock Holmes to *uncover* the counselee – for his or her own sake!

The questioning is a crucial stage – either the first interview aiming to trying to get closer to the native's true time of birth through the events of his/her whole of life up to the moment, and the yearly interview aiming to verify how the previous (Aimed or not, i.e. relocated or not) Solar Return had worked. This latter interrogation has the very same goal, namely the further correction of the counselee's time of birth. A number of enlightening examples on this follow.

Case 1

Male, an expert professional. I suggested him the relocated SR shown in the figure. The year after, he tended to deny the very positive results he had achieved. At the same time he also neglected to point out the undoubtedly negative events that his Aimed SR also showed. In fact, there were positive results, especially concerning an ugly and rare disease which this man suffers from. He was also hired in a company where his specialization gave him direct responsibility over about 700 workers - a really important turning point in his professional life. So far, with many questions and counter–questions, but also with a little cunning, I had managed to pull out from his mouth the information I needed. Yet on one point he was obstinate. I asked him if he had had serious problems with or worries about his brothers, sisters, brothers–in–law, sister–in–law, uncles or cousins or nephews.

With a seemingly unconditional determination, he kept on denying for the entire duration of the session. However, the next day he called me to tell me that, in fact, there was a 'fierce' war going on with his brother because of an inheritance. They were very close to suing each other. Then I wondered why he had professed such a closed – if not obtuse – attitude the previous day, with respect to the examination of a year that had gone splendidly in fact, perfectly fulfilling our expectations (mine and his). The reason that convinced me more (but I could be wrong) was the following.

During the first quarter of an hour of our meeting, he had done nothing but complaining about the birthday journey of the previous year, from a tourist's point of view. He had complained that the agency had cheated him, making him pay big bucks. Perhaps, that bad travel experience might have irritated him a lot. Maybe, unconsciously, he was angry even with me, who had suggested him that year's relocation. This had reached the point of not even letting him see the blatant evidence that he had under his eyes – that of a good year. This is my hypothesis. I have explained other hypotheses of a general nature in my book *Active Astrology* (published in Italy by Edizioni Mediterranee).

But as I mentioned before, it is not the scope of this volume to understand the roots of psychological repression. For our purposes we are only interested in sharpening our technique of questioning.

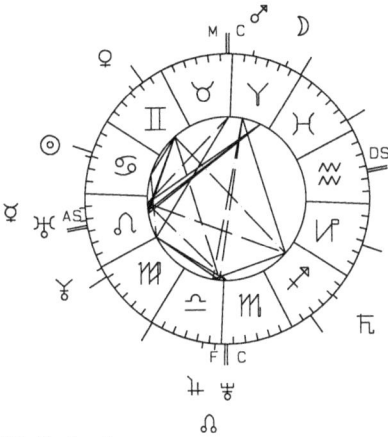

Birth chart

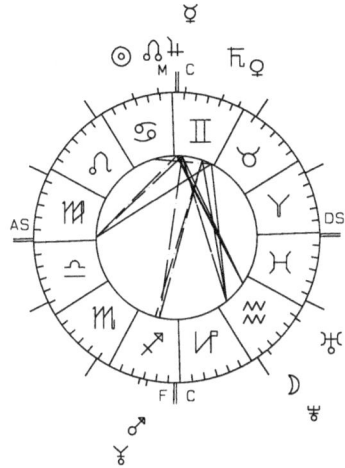

Aimed Solar Return chart

Case 2

This is the case of a rather easy yet interesting procedure of rectification. The official recorded time of birth is 7 pm. At the end of the interview, I corrected it to 6:30 pm. Of course I'm not going to carve it on my personal 'boards of the Bible', but it would be the reference point for future meetings. With a series of several targeted questions, during the interview–interrogation with the counselee, it turned out that he had been carrying on for many years a long–lasting war with a brother–in–law.

This conflict had even led them to file a suite. In addition, he was and still is heavily involved in journalism and publishing. Both facts proved that his natal Mars could not be in the Second House: it should obviously be in his 3rd House. Furthermore, his wife had died suddenly still quite young in age – Uranus must be in his 11th House, not in his 10th.

In the course of his life, he had also been a victim of a theft of considerable proportions. In these cases you can almost always bet on the presence of Jupiter in the natal 2nd or 8th House.

Birth chart, birth time 7:00 pm

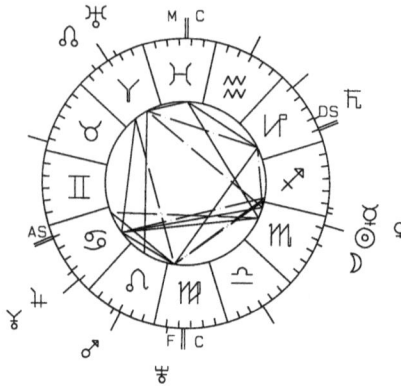

Case 3

This is a lady from our north–eastern region called Veneto. She starts the counselling pretending that her officially recorded time of birth (3:30 am) is obviously wrong, because her father retains a vivid memory of the event. Therefore she claims, "It was 1:30 am!" I cast both charts and I immediately understand that the chart drawn for 1:30 am absolutely does not belong to her. Then I proceed with questions aimed at verifying the official time of birth – 3:30.

If true, as with virtually all the times recorded in the registry, even this time of birth could have been rounded up, say by twenty minutes to half an hour. The answers I get to my questions would demonstrate, in an absolutely conclusive way, that the lady's most likely time of birth – the one possibly closest to the real one – is 3:00 am. The lady's father, in fact, has his Sun in Aquarius, and if she were born around 3:00, the lady's Ascendant would also be Aquarius. She suffers from problems of blood circulation; she underwent surgery to her saphenous vein (mind that we are speaking of objective facts – not statements of moods). She has also hearing problems (Aquarius has much to do with hearing) and suffers from hepatitis C.

And in my experience, if the 1st or the 6th House is heavily occupied by Pisces, this astrological combination can also correspond to this latter specific disease. She was a nurse (almost all of her 1st house is in Pisces)! She also underwent throat surgery (tonsillectomy), has thyroid problems, takes Eutirox (we are talking of facts, not feelings), she sings in a chorus and takes lessons to become an opera singer! Now you tell me – in your opinion does not all this correspond to a stellium in the 3rd or in the 2nd House? Her husband died after only two years of marriage. Moreover – and this could be the final deduction about her time of birth, at least for the first phase: the phase of the interrogation) – recently (this interview takes place in February 2002) her father, mother and her mother–in–law had had serious health problems. At the same time the lady had faced significant expenses for the house. This means that Saturn would have already entered her 4th House, and if not, at least it should transit very close to her Imum Coeli.

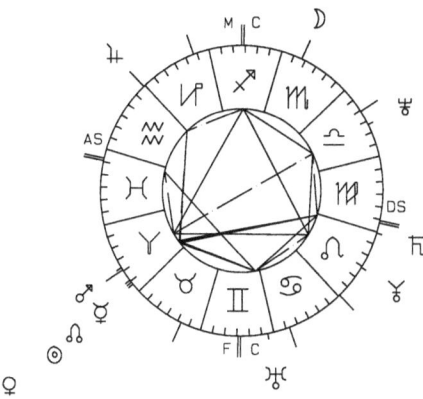

Birth chart, birth time 3:30 am

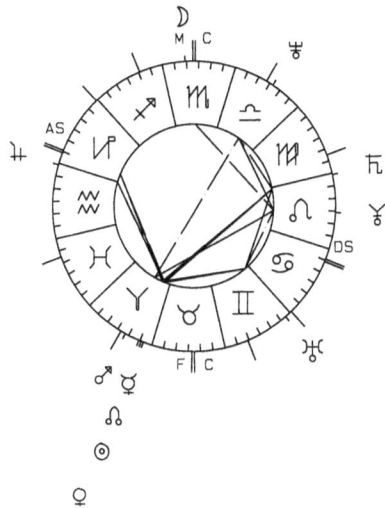

Birth chart, birth time 1:30 am

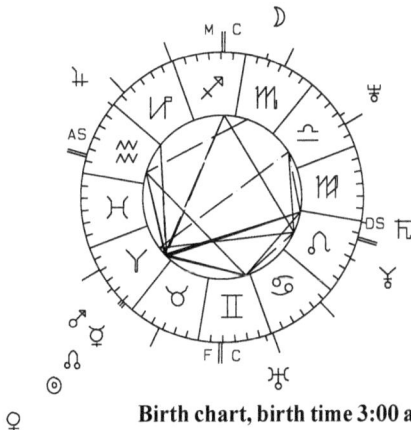

Birth chart, birth time 3:00 am

Case 4

This lady comes asking me to work on her case keeping 0:00 as her true time of birth, despite her birth certificate claiming that she was born at 2:00. In fact, she says, a well–known female colleague astrologer had already rectified her time of birth. I look at both charts and that one cast for midnight can not absolutely match the native and her life. To make a long story short, I eventually consider 1:30 am for the following reasons. As a girl, with an overnight decision she suddenly ran away from home and went to live abroad. Still very young she married her current husband, who is still living. She has a rich and famous brother, who runs a very successful entrepreneurial activity in the field of fashion. She loves driving a car and travelling; she also used to be a heavy smoker – all these clues point to the 3rd House: if the stellium was in the 4th House, how could you explain them?. From a certain point in his life, she could not hire household personnel any longer (Saturn in the 6th House). She is neither separated, nor a widow, nor married to an old husband. I assumed a rectification of her birth record from 2 to 1:30 not only for 'physiological reasons', but also for her physical general aspect, clearly showing Leonine features.

Remember: with the exception of a very few, special cases, we have no reason to doubt the time of birth officially recorded on the native's certificate, except the fact that the official time of birth is usually rounded over in almost all cases.

Also in this case, the stage of interrogation was essential.

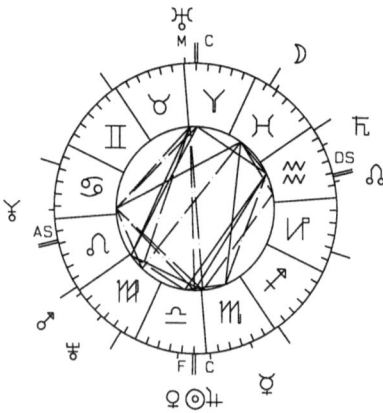

Birth chart, birth time 0:00 am

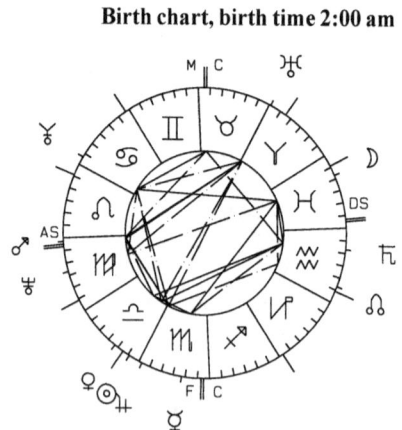

Birth chart, birth time 2:00 am

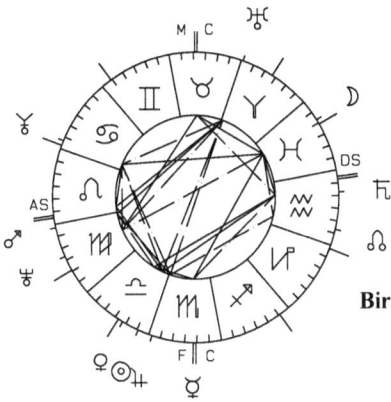

Birth chart, birth time 1:30 am

Case 5

Very brief remarks on this case just to reiterate once again, to what extent the mechanisms of repression can be circuitous. I asked the native whether he had ever had serious heart problems. He replied without hesitation, "Never!". Shortly after, talking with his partner I got to know that in 1995 he had suffered from a heart attack.

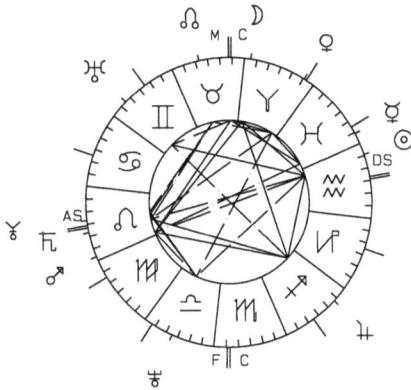

Case 6

Her statement of birth says 11:00, but I immediately suspect that she should be born at about 10:30 am. Here, the visual inspection of the native is extremely important, at least as fundamental as the interrogation. This is a very attractive woman wearing very dark colours and with a certain 'devilish' charm that distinguishes her.

I suspect a very clear rulership of Pluto in her natal chart, which the story of her life obviously confirms. She spent years of torment locked in her house. She had changed several jobs, always with inner pain; she admits that the key word that distinguishes her is 'trouble'.

Her favourite movie is *From Dusk till Dawn* by Quentin Tarantino. If you have watched it, you can not have any more doubts about what I have just written above...

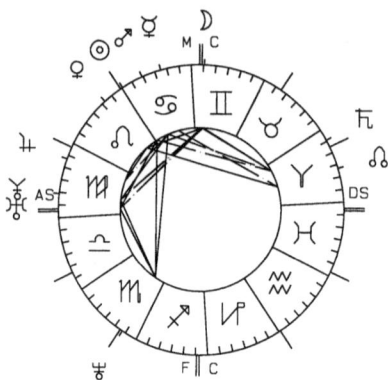

Birth chart, birth time 11:00 am

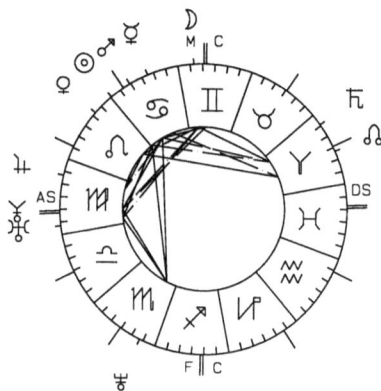

Birth chart, birth time 10:30 am

Case 7

Sardinian male subject who lives in Northern Italy. It's a very interesting case because in this meeting, his repressions were blatant, if not hyperbolic ones. Yet, I must say that he is a reliable person worthy of faith, a respectable man with a strong sense of decency and extremely careful about not hurting others' feelings.

And yet... Trying to establish if indeed the Sun is in his Twelfth House I ask, "Have you ever had problems with your eyes or feet?" He replies, "No, never had anything like this." I insist, "If you don't mind, let us check it out. Were you slightly cross–eyed as a child? Maybe one of your eyes tended to keep a little bit 'closed'? Perhaps, a speck of a different colour in one of your eyes? Have you ever suffered from injuries, accidents, burns, abrasions to the eyes?" He keeps on denying, "Nothing, absolutely nothing!"

"OK, let us talk of your feet. Have you a bunion? You know what a bunion is, don't you? Have you flat feet? Maybe only a little bit? Have you ever worn orthopaedic shoes in your childhood? Have you ever had ingrown toenails? Have your foot ever been injured or burned or broken?" "Nothing, absolutely nothing!"

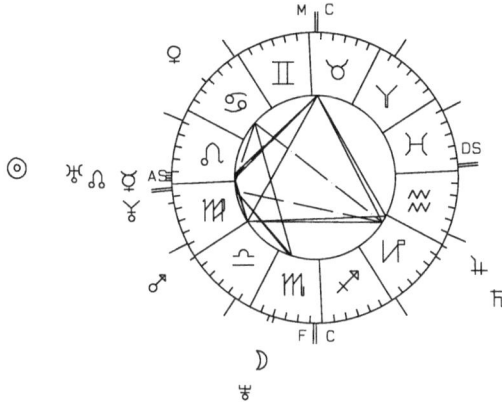

Being an extremely loyal person, half an hour after our chat he calls me and tells me that now he remembers that as a child he had poured bleach into his eyes and keeping it bandaged for a week. The next day he sends me an e–mail apologizing: he is going through a difficult period and is a bit bewildered, he writes. But now, he adds, he can offer me further information concerning the axis eyes–feet. He remembers to have suffered – for a very long time – from a very bad inflammation of the heel. Maybe it wasn't a real inflammation, yet it had prevented him from walking. In addition, two years ago he had broken his foot! And a few weeks before our meeting he had hit his right big toe violently against a wall: it hurt very badly, he writes.

Now just imagine if my questioning had not been so scrupulous and if the person had not been so honest and fair in reporting this additional information!

Case 8

It is a very interesting case of a female from Lazio. She says that the time recorded on her birth certificate is 5:00 pm, but it is certainly a wrong time.

In fact, she has a sister who is eight years older than her, who remembers very well that it was about noon or 1 pm, when the family's dinner had to be postponed because of the birth of her little sister. According to his sister the most likely time of birth is, in fact, sometime around 12. I explain to the lady that it would be very illogical to presume that the day after her birth an aunt or her own father had gone to the Italian registry of births to declare that her birth had taken place at 5 pm while it had actually happened at midday. To be more direct, the father or the aunt who would state so, they should have been immediately hospitalized at the psychiatric hospital. However, I also reassured her: there is no prejudice in me. I told her that I would cast and examine the two possibilities with the same attention, but I would not start either with the chart of 5:00 pm or with the chart of midday. I would start with a third chart instead, cast for 4:30 pm, following the rule that almost thirty years of practice (as in summer 2002) over a large number of cases has taught to me.

As you can see from what follows, my questions have not scanned blindly 360 degrees: they have immediately pointed towards very specific directions.

"Have you relatives born in Libra or Scorpio?"[1]

"My father was a Scorpio; one of my sisters is a Scorpio and the other one is Libra. I also have nephews of Libra and Scorpio."

"Have you personally or a close family member, ever had a serious traffic accident?"

"As a girl, I had one. I had some bad fractures to my jaw, teeth and other parts of my body."

"Maybe one of your brothers or sisters or a brother–in–law or sister–in–law or a niece or a nephew, have been affected by a significant case of misfortune?"

"Well, one of my sisters, two years ago, became ill with throat cancer."

"Have you had any major grief?"

"My father died when I was five. This tragedy has marked my whole life, throwing us in a very precarious financial situation and forcing me to live in different boarding schools."

"Have you ever had one or more love affairs with 'foreigners', I mean, also related to natives of other regions of Italy?"

"Yes, two."

"Have you ever suffered from gynaecological problems?"

"Many, and of different types."

"Have you ever suffered from haemorrhoids?"

"I've just undergone surgery…"

"Have you ever suffered from thyroid?"

"I have nodules and I should take Eutirox, but I disregard it."[2]

"Have you changed more than one job?"

"I have changed a lot of jobs."

"If so, I think there can not be any doubt: you were born certainly very close to 4.30.""

As you can see, if it is true that for two points passes one and only one line, then for ten or more points, all the more so can pass only one and only one line… With regard to the first note [1] please note that in the family of a native whose Ascendant is possibly in Libra you should find a close relative born in that specific sign, and this has been verified.

Birth chart, birth time 12:00 am

Birth chart, birth time 05:00 pm

Birth chart, birth time 4:30 pm

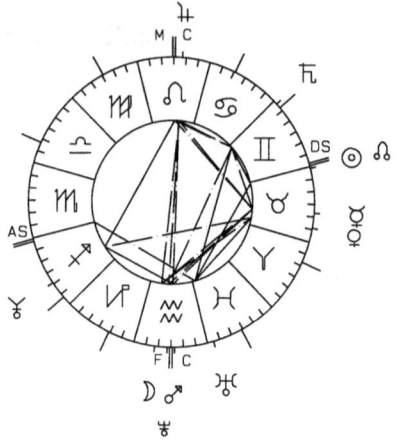

ASR, Brisbane, Australia

Moreover, as I state in my book *Nuova guida all'astrologia* (published in Italy by Armenia editore), I consider that the most important sign is the sign corresponding to the House occupied by the native's Sun (in this case Scorpio). So I also tried to detect a relative born in Scorpio, and it turned out that it was her father – although, of course, I have kept in due consideration that her father being born with the Sun in Scorpio could also be related to the native's Moon in Scorpio. In addition, please also remember the great statistical results obtained by myself and Luigi Miele concerning people's Ascendant: much over the average, one's Ascendant tends to coincide with the solar sign of one of his (or her) parents. It is true that in this case the Ascendant is Libra – but in my opinion, when the cusp lies in Libra 28° and only 1/10 of the 1st House in is Libra, while 9/10 of the House are in Scorpio, this simply proves once again the rule arising from our statistical research on astral heredity, supported by the examination of over 75,000 births.

In connection with the second note [2] please note that at this level I wasn't considering the native's time of birth. I was collecting some other piece of useful information on the native's life. In this case, considering Taurus, I wanted to know whether she also had thyroid problems. I would also mention that her blemished Sun in the 8th House not only could point to a severe loss in the family – it can often be related to significant financial problems (there were, in fact) and to a sort of 'imprisonment' that also had taken place in this lady's life (the boarding school).

I suggested her to relocate her SR of 2003 in Brisbane. Not only would she place a wonderful Jupiter on the MC and an equally splendid Venus in the 6th House as a factual protection to her health. My aim was also to be able to detect which House of SR the Sun and Mars of SR would occupy. In fact, there was a risk that the lady could have had health problems, but she is only about forty years old; so I think it is better to sweep away any further doubt concerning her real time of birth, instead of trying to defer the problem to later years, when the game would have become more dangerous.

Case 9

The native's close relatives swear that he was born at one o'clock in the night, while the verbatim extract of the birth record states 3:00 am. His answers to my first questions, as well as his general aspect, make it appear clear to me that the official recorded time of birth should be the correct one, although it is probably rounded, as it usually happens in all records of birth. He used to sing in a chorus and constantly suffers from throat problems. He also loves a great deal of photography, cinema and theatre. As a young man he had also worked as a film developer in a darkroom. He has always been a little bit unlucky in his emotional life, in his love affairs. In this case, as a starting point which is certainly not the arrival, I guess he may be born at about 2:30 in the morning.

Birth chart, birth time 1:00 am

Birth chart, birth time 3:00 am

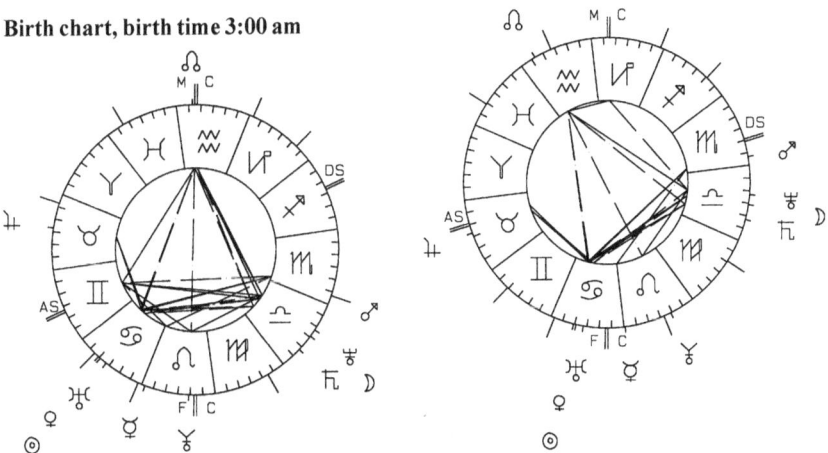

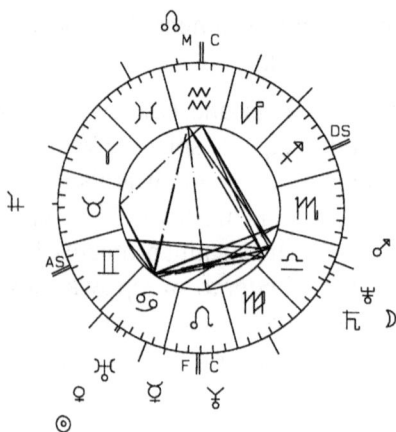

Birth chart, birth time 2:30 am

Case 10

It is not always that the times that are reported should be considered incorrect – it is a good thing to avoid thinking that all the officially recorded times of birth are false. Here is an example that proves what I have just stated. This is a young woman graduated in languages – how could it be otherwise? She comes from a very wealthy family – her birth chart shows a beautiful Venus in the 8th House trine to Jupiter close to the Ascendant. She is tall (Jupiter at the Ascendant), but you must be careful here because this is not an absolute rule: it should always be integrated with the family and local data. Years ago, she suffered from a bad injury to her knee; she also suffers from allergies. But what is perhaps most important, in this case, is the fact that her mother is fond of astrology. Therefore before delivery she asked someone to register the time of the event with the accuracy of the minutes: 12:40.

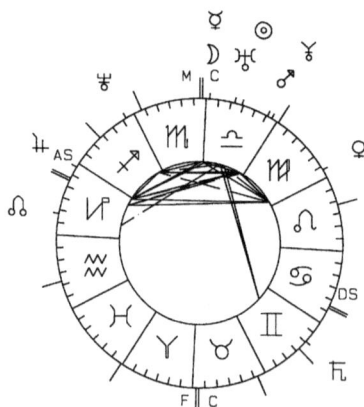

Birth chart

Case 11

"Have you personally or has a close family member, ever had trouble with the law?"

"My grandfather had, many years ago; he suffered a failure that changed his life."

"And what about you? Has it never happened that you experienced anything unpleasant in this field?"

"No, never."

"Let me see, for example, maybe you had a dispute with the police which led to an indictment?"

"Well, yes, as a boy I quarrelled with a couple of Carabineers who had stopped my car, I got a little bit angry with them. This caused me a criminal complaint, but then everything turned to nothing..."

"Am I right if I say that in your life, the field of romantic relationships and/or social relationships has always been your 'wooden spoon', the most troublesome aspect of your life?"

"Certainly! I had four major affairs, including a wedding, and they all ended badly. I also had a society, but with two members it also ended badly."

"Has your throat been a source of trouble for you?"

"Always." (He is particularly thin.)

"Do you love music and singing?"

"No."

"Do you mean that you don't like listening to music? That you have never ventured to sing or play an instrument?"

"No, what I mean is that I do like both things – but music is not at the top of my interests."

"Can you tell me what other positive link exists, if any, between you and your throat, gluttony?"

"Well I deal with food, especially as a journalist and essayist, and also appear frequently on television."

"One last question. You told me you have two daughters: maybe one or both of them came in a sudden, unexpected way?"

"Both of them, I'd say."

As you have surely understood, my questioning was aiming to demonstrate that the native was born earlier than the given time, thus his Sun lies in the 2nd house and Uranus in the 5th House. Furthermore that awful stellium of Mars, Saturn and Pluto is definitely, completely contained in his Seventh House.

I have temporarily rectified his time to five o'clock, waiting for new checks.

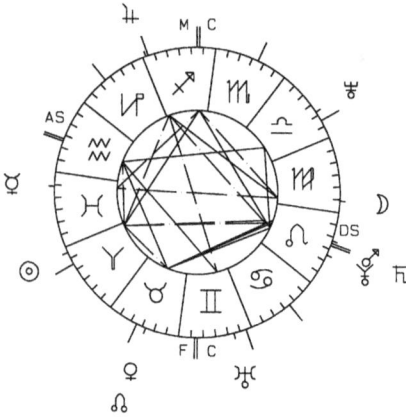

Birth chart, birth time 5:30 am

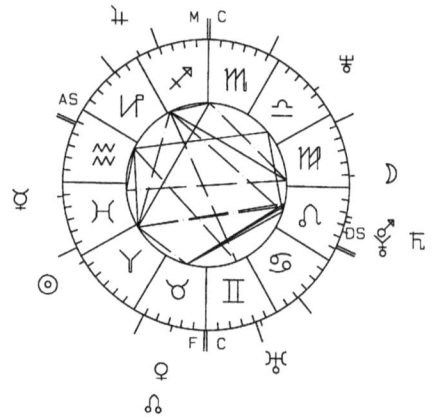

Birth chart, birth time 5:00 am

Case 12

Female, from central Italy. According to her, she was born at 4 pm, and this time of birth is confirmed in fact both by her mother and by her official record. Nonetheless this does not convince me at all because she comes from a peasant family with many children.

She occupies a prominent place in public administration; she behaves in a certain way and expresses character traits and behaviours that make me think she is a Capricorn. For the time being it is only one clue, but I decide to follow it, asking, "Have you close relatives of Capricorn?"

"Yes, my father."

"Have you ever suffered significantly due to troubles with your teeth, bones and knees in particular?"

"In all three things, yes."

"Could you prove, with factual evidence and not only with words, that you are very ambitious?"

"I put my career ahead of everything – that's why I have recently separated."

Just to be certain, I ask other questions but my mind is already clear.

"Has your father ever had an accident of some importance?"

"My father died many years ago. When he was alive he had more than one serious accident at work, he had a small enterprise dealing with house building."

"Have you made your fortune far from your place of birth?"

"Yes, in another region of Italy."

"You have already told me of your divorce. But can I say that you have very few friends?"

"Yes, you know: true friends can be counted on one hand."

At this point I have made my decision: I move the time to 3:20 pm, so that the Ascendant lies in the last degrees of Capricorn. Later on, of course, I would try to show how this is possible.

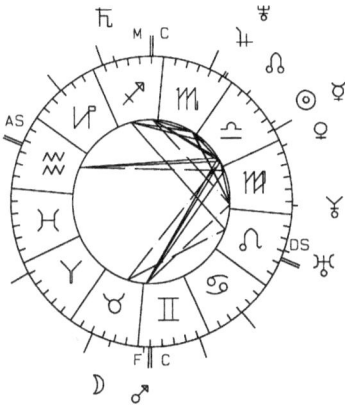

Birth chart, birth time 4:00 pm

Birth chart, birth time 3:20 pm

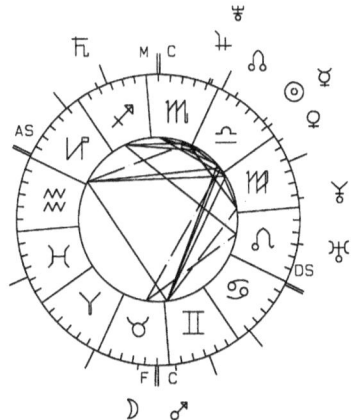

Case 13

Male subject, freelance, from insular Italy. First he tells me that he was born between 8:30 and 8:45; then – after questioning his mother – he asks me to work with 8:20 as his true time of birth. Several traits of his person as well as his first sentences make me think that his natal Sun lies in the Twelfth House. I detect natives of Pisces in his family tree. In addition, in the past he was in charge of giving assistance to his grandparents. He also used to adopt several pets from the streets to take care and look after them, until he got married.

When I asked if he feels persecuted by life and fate, he starts a long speech to convince me to be very unlucky; that everything goes wrong without him being able to counteract somehow this basic existential bad luck.

He also had problems in the eyes and feet.

I move the Sun just below the line of the Twelfth House. Later, I would try to find out more.

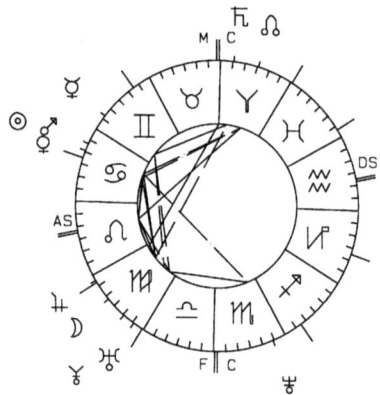

Birth chart, birth time 8:20 am

Case 14

It is a very interesting and difficult case, but it could help you understand many things.

This is a male from Campania; a young–looking and pleasant man. His birth certificate says he was born at 4:40 pm, but something just does not convince me after a long and well–structured interrogation.

First of all, the visual inspection. As I said, he looks much younger than he actually is. He smiles frequently and naturally. His conversation is nice and lively. He has fast response times, he interrupts me often, he frequently hops from one subject to another, he has what they call 'anticipatory anxiety'

– he would like to thank in advance of receiving a gift. Furthermore his physiognomy resembles a Gemini rather than a Cancer (obviously I am referring to his the Ascendant). In fact, many people belonging to the fourth sign of the zodiac has their face resembling an owl, a night bird, similar in many ways to the current chairman of *RCS* Cesare Romiti or to the television quiz champion Massimo Inardi (who was very famous in the seventies). They frequently wear eyeglass with heavy frames, which are more like frames of old pictures than supports for lenses.

The person before me does not have any of these characteristics. In addition, he smokes two packs of cigarettes a day – a fact that goes almost without saying for a solar Gemini or an Ascendant Gemini. Well, some people may be wondering, *What's the matter then?* In fact, the first chess move I tried to make was to bring back his time of birth by 15–20 minutes. But there was a hindrance. From our long interview, by way of objective facts and not for alleged unrealized dreams or aspirations, it appeared clear that he is a lawyer. He also was an active militant in politics. He had experienced three total failures in his only three love affairs of his life. One of these failures has been a divorce; the other two were long cohabitations eventually and definitely discontinued.

He is also a person of good taste; he is very sensitive to injustice, even though his character is not at all belligerent as his conjunction of Sun–Moon–Mars may suggest. Maybe someone would still be wondering where the problem or the difficulty in solving this case is. I tell you right now. He claims – but we would soon see that this matches an important experience of his life; it is not just vague illusions – that his passion is represented by all those practices of shiatsu and/or smooth manipulation where he can have a sort of medical influence on the others.

He has been dealing with it for decades and he is presently leaving his career of a lawyer to devote time entirely to his true passion – and this is where the anomaly is! This second aspect of his personality can be explained only with a Sun in the Sixth House! No other part of his chart could even remotely justify such a strong interest in medicine and body care of others through manipulative techniques. Therefore, I found myself at an apparent dead end, with no logical solutions to unravel the mystery.

But, as I said, I think I have found an explanation that would teach you many things about astrology and especially on this particular facet, which by my express desire is devoted to the problem of correcting the time of birth mainly through an *interrogation*. What I am going to explain now is my solution to this puzzling case – the solution in which I believe. However, I am willing to reconsider it if future events, the other techniques that I would put in place with him or a convincing explanation of a colleague astrologer will ever prove things differently from those that I have found.

I think that he was actually born at 4.30 pm, one minute less or more. For if that were the case, he would have the Ascendant on the last degree of Gemini. Even if the First House lies almost completely in Cancer, the very evident traces of Gemini would not disappear, starting the two very practical packs of cigarettes that he has been smoking every day for over twenty years. At this point, Mars would be quite high over the Descendant; and his natal Sun would still be over Descendant, but closer – approximately two degrees from the cusp. Now it seems that we are really dealing with a textbook case in which all theories of this world, all the theoretical formulations of the astrologers, including my own, must necessarily be bowing to reality: if a celestial is close to a cusp, it may 'work' in both Houses.

The measure that I have myself indicated several times is 2°30'.

I believe that this case may represent a milestone in proving this.

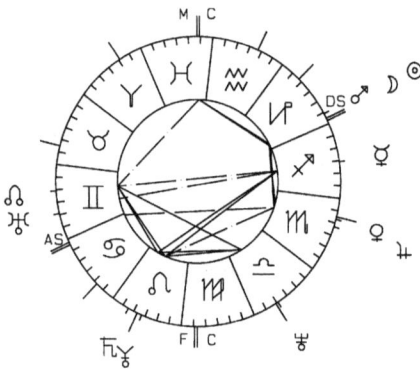

Birth chart, birth time 4:30 pm

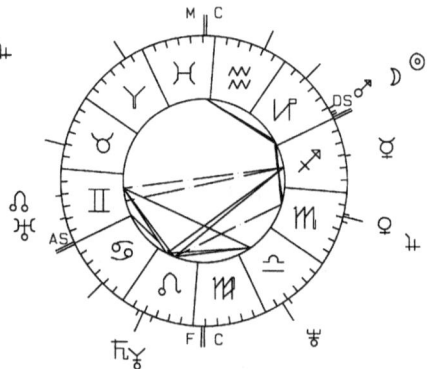

Birth chart, birth time 4:40 pm

Case 15

This is a case that, like few others, allows you to establish within the range of minutes, and with a very high degree of certainty, the true time of birth of the counselee – who in this case is a male, born and raised in Campania.

He has a small business in the field of handmade / industrial products and has suffered two major 'robberies' in his life. The first time, many years ago his incapability of managing a commercial business caused a state of bankruptcy, which led him to sacrifice an apartment and a shop to compensate for the debt. The second time, recently, he was denied the proceeds of a compensation for the death of his child in a car accident. A car had cut across the boy's path, but the judge closed the investigation in a few days without even a verdict of contributory negligence. Due to other legal grounds, it was not possible to file an appeal, thus my counselee lost a possible compensation running into billions.

From my interrogation I also got to know of his second wife's death. He also smokes very much, he loves to drive the car, he looks extremely young and has a daughter born in the sign of Leo. He has a definitely *Leonine* look himself. Both his parents' memories and the official statement of birth say that he was born at 2:30, but it seems quite clear that he should be born at 2:15 instead – one minute more or one minute less. In fact, rectifying his time back by a quarter of an hour, you can find that his Ascendant is in Leo and his Sun lies in the Third House – the latter position confirming his strong Gemini–like features such as his looking much younger, his tendency to smoke a lot, his pleasure of driving a car and so on. But if you went further back in time you would make his Saturn leave his natal Eighth House, which has clearly played a major role in his life – two deaths and two major important economic losses – moreover, you would not even find any track of the terrible traffic accident that killed his son.

For these reasons – without having any pretension of carving anything on the boards of the Bible – I am confident that his time of birth is close to 2:15.

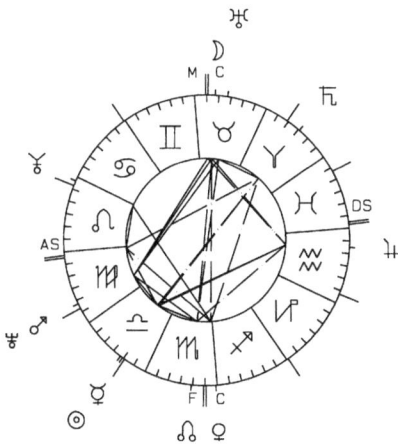

Birth chart, birth time 2:30 am

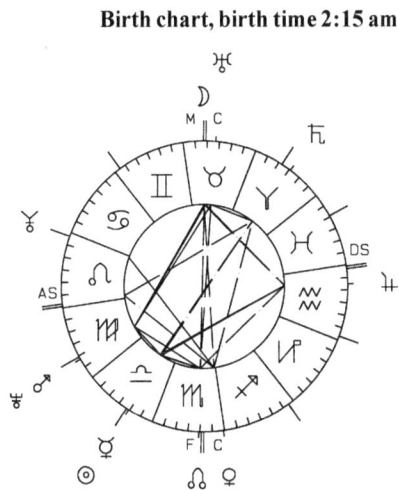

Birth chart, birth time 2:15 am

Case 16

This is another case, and a quite rare one, where you can almost certainly detect in a few minutes a narrow _range_ of oscillation in the native's time of birth. In this case he is a male who works as a manager in the North–East of Italy. Of course we start from a declared time of birth at 6 pm, accurate to the minute! My first two questions found directly its target.

"Is there anyone of Virgo in your family?"

"Yes, there is."

"Has one of your brothers or a sister or a brother–in–law or a sister–in–law have ever had serious problems with drug addiction or suffered from significant neurosis?"

"Yes, both my brother and my sister–in–law have had a history of drug addiction."

At this point, several other questions follow confirming this type of input. Then I try to determine whether his natal Jupiter lies in the 10th or in the 11th House. It is not an easy thing to find out, but from a precise sequence of answers I gather that he arrived quickly to a stage of great professional success on his own steam, and not by external support.

At this point, if he were born half an hour earlier, he would have Jupiter on the cusp of the Eleventh House – which I consider to be impossible. Conversely, if I consider a birth at 5:45 pm – but I also accept a range of ten to twenty–five minutes before 6 pm – I get Neptune in the Third House and Jupiter surely in the 10th House. In the future I'll consider this latter time of birth with the utmost attention.

Birth chart, birth time 6:00 pm

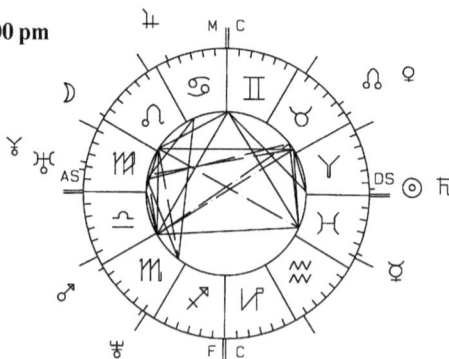

Birth chart, birth time 5:30 pm

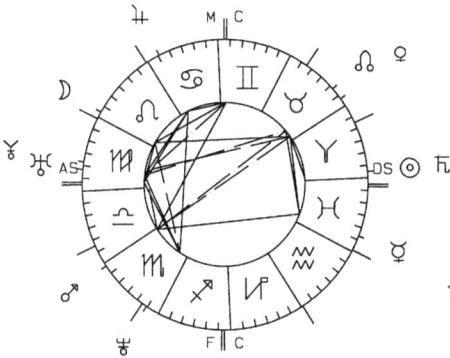

Birth chart, birth time 5:45 pm

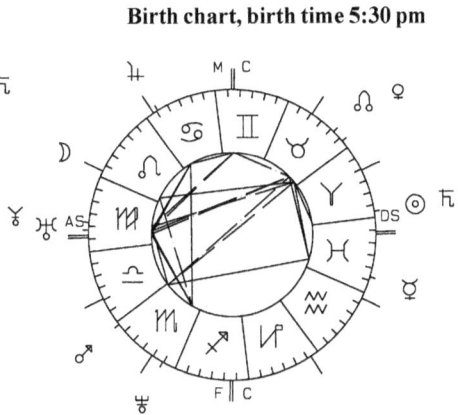

Case 17

Female subject from Liguria, unmarried. Both her birth certificate and her parents state that her time of birth is 7:30 pm. Through many specific questions, I try to see whether her natal Sun is in the 5th or 6th House.

"Do you often go out at night?"

"It depends."

"OK, let us put it this way. Consider that you were referring to the average of all years since you were a girl until today and, possibly, without declaring your expectations, but only facts. For example, exclude contingent causes during this period that would prevent you from going out often in the evening, I would like you to tell me something like this: *I go out on average four times a week.*"

"In fact I go out, on average, exactly 4 to 5 times a week."

"Where do you go or what do you do when you go out at night?"

"It depends."

"In the majority of cases where do you go and what do you do?"

"Certainly I go to dance, to the disco and to places where there is music and lots of people."

"Are you, or have you ever been a gambler? Have you ever played poker, roulette or similar?"

"Yes, I used to, even for long periods. But I always played such games where luck might depend more directly on me than on anything 'distant'.

For example I like playing poker because there I can have a recitative reactive role, while I do not like to do the football pools, because it looks like mere chance – it's away from me and I cannot have any control on it."

"All this suggests that you may have the Sun in the 5th House, but let us do the double check to see if your Sun is in the 6th House instead. Objectively, can you say that you have good manual skills? Can you do something 'special' with your hands?"

"People tell that I am very good at massaging."

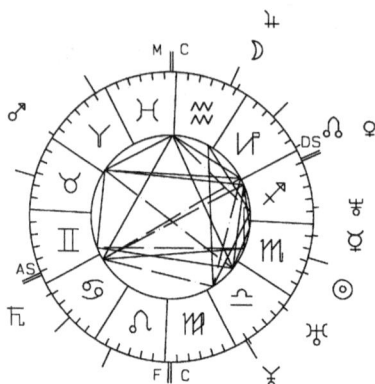

Birth chart, birth time 7:30 pm

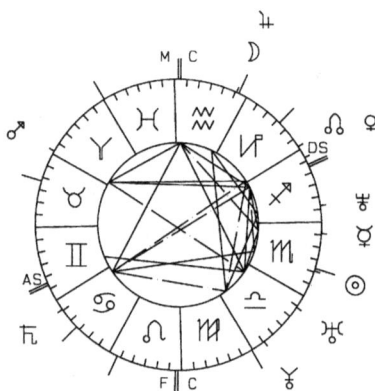

Birth chart, birth time 7:15 pm

This latter question is aimed to differentiate, already at the beginning, the area of a possible medical *libido* from that of an artistic nature. For those who have the Sun in the Sixth House and have good manual skills can usually take two main paths to make a professional use of them or just as a hobby. The first way is the medical or paramedical field – doing massages, shiatsu or enrolling in courses of reiki and so on – while the other is the field of craft / art, maybe painting, making sculptures, restorations or similar art–related activities. Since the counselee herself had given me a good clue, I tried to verify it.

"Am I right if I say that you are a bit hypochondriacal? And if you agree, can you demonstrate it with facts?"

"Yes, indeed, I am. The first thing that I wanted to say to you is, *do not make me aware of any illnesses that may affect me.* I often ask the doctor to visit me and I always live with the anguish of falling severely ill. I also try to lead a fairly healthy life."

As you can see, she could produce enough objective evidence which suggest that her Sun was exactly on the cusp between the Fifth and the Sixth House. So, for the time being, I advance her time of birth to 7.15 pm, waiting for further observation of future facts in her life.

Case 18

It is a very interesting situation. A male subject, who lives in an island of Italy. He has a job in the commercial field. His birth record says 11 o'clock, while his mother vows to remember that it was 6:30. I have to make a digression at this point. I admit that I usually start with the following prejudice: I feel much more comfortable with the time officially recorded than the time given by the parents. On the other hand, there is also a second prejudice guiding my interrogation: always doubt my own beliefs. For I am convinced that if I was not very suspicious – *mistrustful* to use a quite difficult word for an Italian – before everything, everybody, and even myself, the results of my investigation would be mush less reliable.

The digression is over; let us stick to this case. I begin with asking a series of questions to ascertain the reliability of the official time of birth, 11:00. The man has no relative of Taurus. However, he suffers from hoarseness and he is very thin, a very *Taurine* thinness. However, apart from that nothing seems to be matching anything related to the sign Taurus. In fact, he has not undergone any major or tragic mourning; neither relatives nor close friends have died around him (despite his Mars and Saturn being in the Eleventh House). He has not even had memorable arguments in his life. Furthermore he has no children; he has not had one or more of his partners having abortions; he has never wished to have an offspring. As a boy he was interested in photography, film and similar techniques, but all this remained only in terms of vocations – nothing more. At this point, I suspect that his time of birth can be wrong; I cast another chart 6:30 and make questions concerning the latter chart.

As you may remember, one of my statistical researches, conducted together with Luigi Miele on over 75,000 births, was striving to show how frequently people's Ascendant falls into the solar sign of one of their parents. And in fact it turns out immediately that his mother is a Capricorn! And – hear ye – one of his knees hurts because of a car accident dating back from several years before. He has also dental problems (he claims to have *always* been under dental care) as well as problems with his bones. So could you not recognize an Ascendant in the sign of Capricorn? Nonetheless, I seek further confirmation.

"Do you suffer from stomach problems?", I ask aiming at both the Ascendant in Capricorn and the Sixth House in Cancer.

"Yes, I have gastritis. They wanted me to undergo gastroscopy, but I refused!"

"Have you ever been particularly lucky with occasional love affairs, flirts, flings?"

"Surely I am lucky."

"Could your mother be called a 'very religious' or 'very neurotic' woman?"

"Yes, both definition matches reality."

At this point everything is coherent including the mosaic tile concerning his aborted vocation in the field of photography and films. In fact, in this hypothesis of time of birth, you can find Saturn in the Second House – not Jupiter!

However, there is another point that at first glance would not seem to figure, namely his chronic pharyngitis and excessive thinness. But if you accept this latter time of birth, you detect a dominant Venus conjunct with the Ascendant, which has certainly the same meaning as an Ascendant in Taurus. To make a long story short, at this point there cannot be any more doubt. I would accept the time of birth stated by the mother, with the only rectification of advancing it by a quarter of hour for the time being to 6:15.

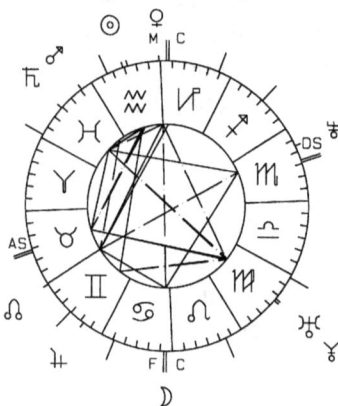

Birth chart, birth time 11:00 am

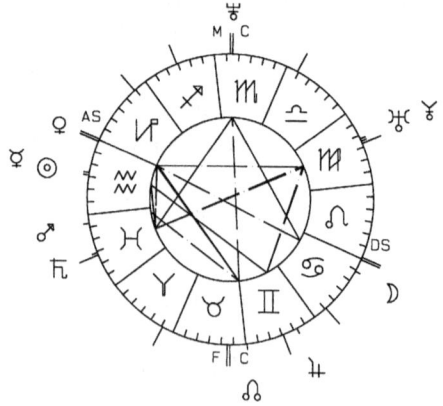

Birth chart, birth time 6:30 am

Case 19

This is another fairly simple case of correction of the time of birth. It is a young male, enrolled in a course of architecture. The time is confirmed both by his mother and by the official record: 7:45 pm. But it can not be so. My suspicion is that the Ascendant lies in Virgo, not Libra. This notion acquires greater force when he tells me that one of the parents – namely his mother – was born in the sign of Virgo. He is also a student on architecture, he draws very well, he paints and he has excellent manual skills. The data seem to be so objective that it is impossible not to amend his time of birth a little back in time. But by how much? Not much, for the following two reasons.

1) His mother's memory and the official record point to the very same time of birth: this leads you to think that you must not stray too far from the time declared.

2) After a series of other questions, I detect that his parents are separated. The young man considers his mother as one of the positive points of his life. He can also give objective evidence of his mother supporting all the moments of spiritual growth he has experienced in the past.

In short, I think (without ever filing this case as definitive) that his Ascendant should be in Virgo and his Jupiter in the Tenth House. Perhaps he is born a quarter of an hour before 7:45, with the ascendant at the very last degree of the sixth sign of the Zodiac.

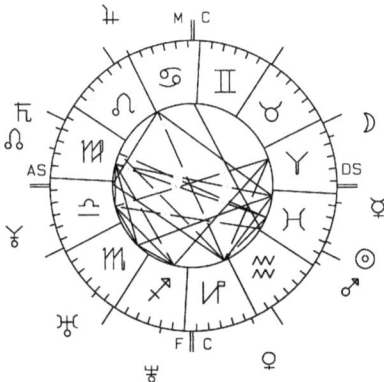

Birth chart, birth time 7:45 pm

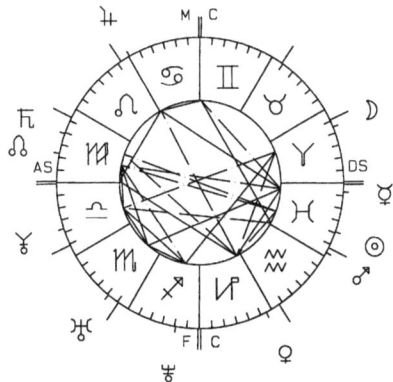

Birth chart, birth time 7:30 pm

Case 20

Here is an example of the 'mythologies' that sometimes can accompany the birth of a man, setting the astrologer on the wrong track in his verifying the true time of birth. This is a woman from Northern Italy, born on the 22nd of November, 1963. Her mother claims that she had made the first cry exactly at the very moment when John Fitzgerald Kennedy was shot in Dallas. These are her words: "It was 10 am in Dallas; therefore it was 4 pm here in Italy. My mother remembers it well because there was a TV set where she was giving birth – exactly at that moment they were broadcasting the live coverage of JFK's murder."

Now, let me start by saying that the thirty–fifth U.S. president, who ruled from 1961 to 1963, was killed in Dallas precisely at 12:30 pm Central Standard Time. Therefore, here in Italy it was 7.30 pm – not 4 pm. Furthermore, the lady's birth certificate states she was born at 10 pm. Therefore I cast a birth chart for the latter time of birth and I start questioning the lady considering this chart. Her answers do not help me much. She does not remember the signs of all the members of her family tree. She is also confused about the dates.

I was attempting to detect whether she had relatives born in Sagittarius, which would have confirmed to me that the lady's Ascendant falls in Sagittarius – but this attempt fails. She does not even remember her own mother's solar sign. All she knows is that her mother died young, that she used to be a little bit depressed, neurotic, and an extremely religious woman (a churchy one). Her mother also overindulged in drinks. All these elements confirm the native's Neptune in her natal 10th House. At the most, since her mother died of cirrhosis, these elements may also corroborate the hypothesis of the lady's Ascendant lying in Sagittarius. Nonetheless, I prefer to rely on facts, not on assumptions. So I consider that the lady is a sportsperson. This may possibly confirm her Ascendant in Sagittarius. I get positive answers when I ask if she has ever suffered at the teeth, bones and knees. She convincingly gives affirmative answers on all these three points. Therefore her Ascendant may be lying at the end of the sign of Sagittarius and her 1st House may include a good portion of Capricorn. She confesses a very strong love for music, which may match her Sun lying in the natal 11th House. In addition, she also dresses in a quite original way. She gives clearly the impression of being more like a native of Aquarius than Scorpio – this would be consistent with her Sun lying in the Eleventh House.

Her husband suffers from severe psychological problems. She also had a long–lasting episode of psychosis once, which would authorize me to maintain her conjunction Mars–Venus in the Twelfth House.

There can not be the least doubt on the fact that she has a… 'rotten luck' in her economic–commercial activities. In fact, she owns a small store that is leading her quickly to bankruptcy because of the debts accumulated over many years.

But the nice thing about the interview happens when I ask her if she drives a car. "No, not at all!", she claims. Her answer keeps me puzzled: since the lady's education is quite poor and she takes no interest at all in reading or studying, her Sagittarian features should express itself at least in a significant interest for cars. So I insist on this point.

"I see. So you're telling me that if you won a large sum at the Lottery you would not spend even a small portion of that amount in purchasing good-looking car, would you?"

"No, on the contrary, my first major expense would be to buy a Mercedes or even a Ferrari…"

"So I do not understand why you've just told me that you don't like driving a car."

"I do not like driving a car because I have a horrible, old and shabby wreck. But if I had another car, a new and luxurious one, I'd be driving all day."

The provisional time of birth I consider is therefore 9:30, which would correspond to an Ascendant on the cusp between Sagittarius and Capricorn. Once again, this example gives you the opportunity to reflect on the following two issues: on the one hand, *mythologies* and on the other hand, *false answers*.

With regard to mythologies it is fairly easy to see how things could have happened in this case. Probably it all started with her mother, who was an alcoholic among other things, referring to everybody – and with great emphasis – that her daughter was born the very same day of Kennedy's death. Then, almost certainly, months and years passed by, and probably with an unconscious and involuntary process, her mother began to tell that the birth took place at the exact time of the murder. But by claiming so she made a little bit of mess, and if you add the time difference between the USA and Italy, the story got totally mixed up.

Although rounded up as in the majority of cases, the officially recorded time of birth matches the factual reality.

The second issue concerns lies, or false information that everybody could give you during the interview. In this case, if I had accepted the lady's answer concerning the car, without any further questioning, I'd probably gone off the track; and maybe this nice lady would also have been be able to convince me that she was born at the very instant when the bullets whistled in Lee Harvey Oswald's or somebody else's ear...

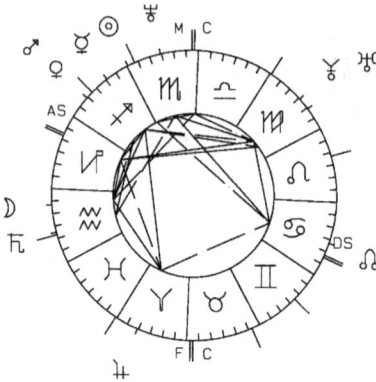

Birth chart, birth time 10:00 am

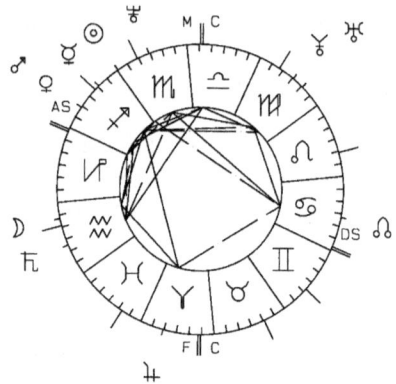

Birth chart, birth time 9:30 am

Case 21

This is a rather simple case of a male subject from Piedmont. The extract of his birth record states 1:15 am while on a book compiled shortly after delivery, his mother wrote 1:15 pm. Both parents and almost all his close relatives are long dead, so they can not enlighten me about his true time of birth. The logic suggests that the birth actually took place at 1:15 pm, and whoever went personally to state the birth to the registry simply said '1:15'. The declarer meant, 'pm', the officer understood, 'am'. Nonetheless, one should never make things too simple. Always try to find 'fairly objective' evidence of your suppositions.

So I ask, "Have you close relatives of Pisces or Virgo?"

"Both signs – my father was Pisces and my daughter, Virgo."

Unluckily this does not help me at all.

"Have you or your immediate family ever had road accidents of a certain significance?"

"If the fact that my father died in a car accident matches what you mean, then the answer is *yes*."

This would also explain the presence of Saturn on the Descendant in one of the two charts. So I ask, "Have you ever suffered from some sort of 'war' or other problems with the law?"

"I had a long dispute with my brothers and my sisters because of an inheritance."

"Have you good manual skills?"

"At home I like to do many small jobs; I can also paint furniture, doors, etc."

"Have you ever had diseases or other problems in your hands?"

"I have a couple of fairly large cysts on the back of my hand."

At this point it seems obvious to me that I can credit 1:15 pm to be the true time of birth of this man, with the Ascendant lying in Virgo.

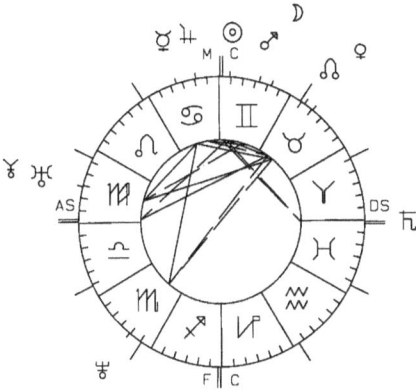

Birth chart, birth time 13:15 pm

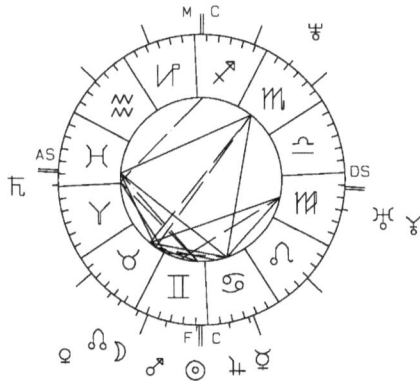

Birth chart, birth time 1:15 pm

Case 22

The rewards are satisfying, but when they are certified they are even more pleasant. This female from Campania is a businesswoman in the field of fashion. She designs, creates and produces garments. The time of birth remembered by her parents is 8:00 am.

Cast for that time, her birth chart matches in all respects the lady's character, but – given the fact that almost all of the times of birth are rounded up and given also the fact that she is a very attractive and charming woman, who is a fashion artist – I think, I am quite confident that she should be born with her Venus conjunct to the Ascendant. I ask her to produce her extract of birth record. The officially recorded time of birth is

7:40, which corresponds to a Venus exactly conjunct with the Ascendant!

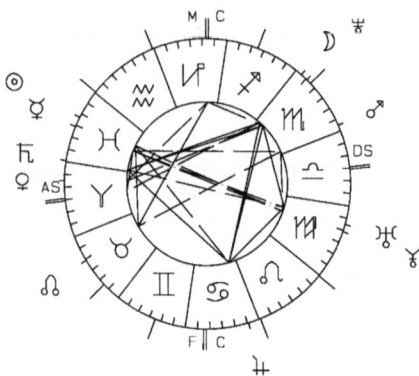

Birth chart, birth time 7:40 am

Birth chart, birth time 8:00 am

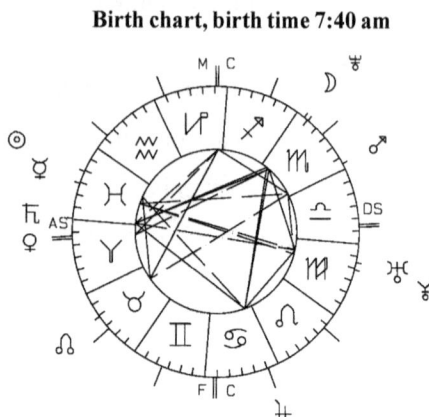

Case 23

This case is particularly interesting. The man is a television director in Northern Italy. His parent swore (his father is dead) that his time of birth is 1:50 pm. I think that even in this case I am facing the usual ten–to–fifteen–minute rounding and I start making my questions, but nothing seems to match. So I start considering the chance that the time of birth could much earlier in fact, so I go on questioning in a targeted way.

"You have undergone many surgeries or accident or fractures, haven't you?"

"Only tonsillectomy."

This question was primarily intended to exclude, with a certainty of virtually 100%, that his terrible natal conjunction was located in the First House.

"Have you personally, or a close relative of yours, ever experienced a dramatic financial span of time?"

"Yes, my father lent much money to relatives and we found ourselves in poverty, almost overnight."

You've told me that you underwent throat surgery. Does your throat still ache, frequently?"

"Yes, it's one of my weak points."

"Have you ever suffered from small forms of bulimia and/or anorexia?"

"Very often indeed."

"Is there anything else that you can tell me of your throat? Smething positive, I mean."

"I love singing very much."

"Before taking to directing TV programmes, have you ever had anything to do with films, frames, etc.?"

"Yeah, pretty much – I would say, I have *always* been dealing with such things."

At this point I do not think there can be any doubt whatsoever. His deadly opposition of celestials must necessarily be in the 2nd and 8th House – not between the 1st and the 7th.

For the time being I rectify his time of birth to 1:00 pm.

Please note that this man has also problems with sight. In my books I have been exposing plenty of evidence to demonstrate that serious problems in the eyes or vision are related with the Pisces–Virgo axis, and this is just one of the many cases confirming this rule.

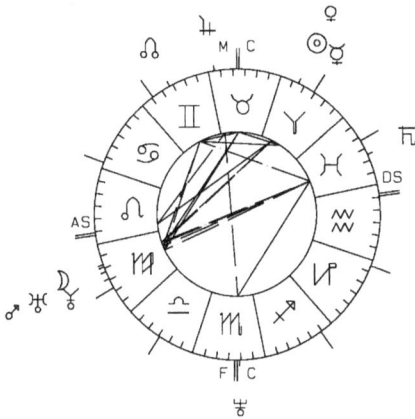

Birth chart, birth time 1:00 pm

Birth chart, birth time 1:50 pm

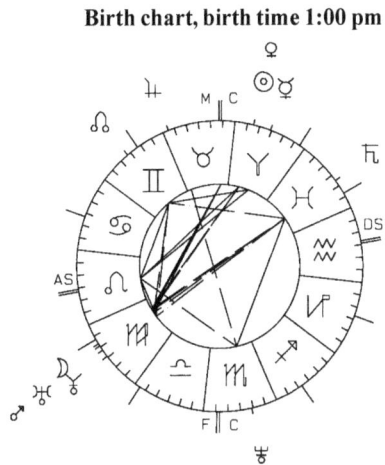

Case 24

Female subject from Tuscany. The time indicated by her parents is 9 am.

I first try to get evidence that her Sun really lies in the Twelfth House, and in fact I find many elements that are consistent with it: one of her grandfathers was Pisces, she suffer from various problems with her eyes and foot; she also shows slightly 'paranoid' tendencies, probably justified by an objective amount of bad luck in her life.

So I try to understand whether it is possible to rectify her time of birth to half an hour earlier, so that her natal Jupiter lies in the 2nd House. I start questioning about her financial situation, but her answers do not match the typical features of a Jupiter in the 2nd House. For example she has never been robbed, she has never lost money by accident, she does not even love photography and cinema; and she has no other feature that may be consistent with Jupiter in the Second House. While it is plausible to think that Jupiter lies in her 1st natal House because she had a very bright career, at least at its beginnings. Therefore, for the time being, I fix her provisional rectified time of birth at 8:45.

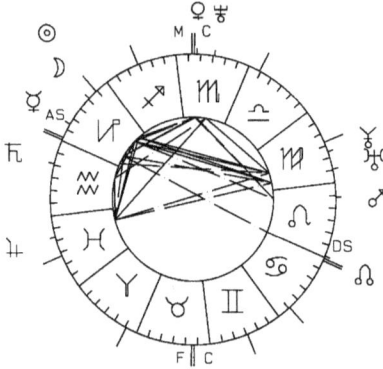

Birth chart, birth time 9:00 am

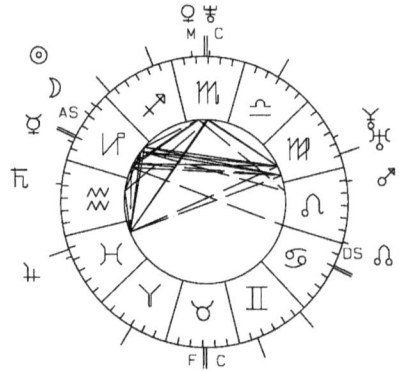

Birth chart, birth time 8:30 am

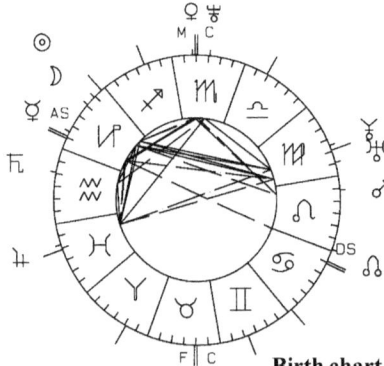

Birth chart, birth time 8:45 am

Case 25

I think that those who opt to help others through astrology (the same also refers to medicine, psychology and many other disciplines) must continually take as a reference point a sort of *Hippocratic Oath*, as in the case of doctors. And in any case, they must be prepared to do their utmost to be always as tolerant as possible.

However, sometimes there are people who do their utmost to try your nerves, as in the following case.

This is a male from central Italy who declares that his time of birth is 4 pm, confirmed by the memory of some aunts. Despite the declared time of birth, from the preliminary questions and answers I understand that his natal Sun must inevitably be lying in his 8th House and Mars in the 4th House. When he was very young, one of his parents died of cancer, and two years later the other one also died of cancer. His mother died of a malignant breast tumour. This man's Ascendant is Cancer and there might be a relationship with her mother's solar sign, but he does not remember any of the zodiac signs of his relatives. His father was hospitalized for an accident and was kept in hospital for further diagnosis. He died there due to liver cancer a few weeks later.

His grandfather took care of him and his brother, but then he also had a serious accident which confined him to a wheelchair with an amputated leg. Shortly after, his grandfather died. The two children changed many houses; in each one of them they experienced bereavement or a very unfortunate incident.

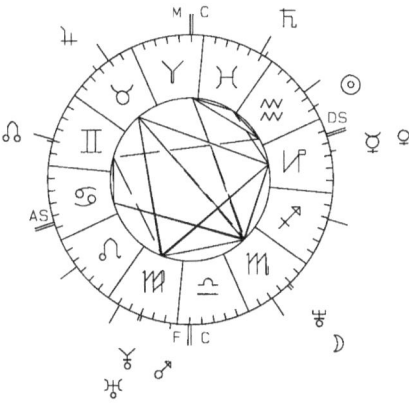

Birth chart, birth time 3:30 pm

Birth chart, birth time 4:00 pm

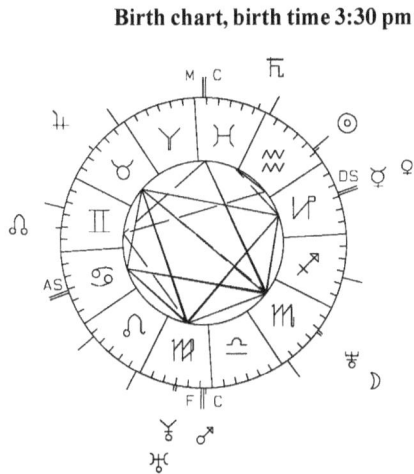

Finally, they were 'adopted' by a wealthy family, who has been taking care of them since then, and who still represent perhaps the only positive reality for this very unfortunate orphan (Jupiter in the Eleventh House). He is unfortunate but stubborn, because when I tried to explain that everything, absolutely everything in his chart is consistent with Sun in the Eighth House and Mars in the 4th House, he insisted that he could not be born even a minute before 4 o'clock only because their aunts swore so! So, without losing patience and without being aggressive, I calmly replied, "Well, I believe what you are saying and in this case I have to give you the good news: your parents are not deceased and even your grandfather lives. In addition, both your father and grandfather have never had serious accidents and you have never moved in dramatic circumstances."

Then, of course, I explained better. I made it clear that I didn't mean to be sarcastic or ironic concerning such distressing events. Eventually this man realized that it is necessary to believe more in the stars than in human beings!

For the time being I put his birth clock back half an hour.

Case 26

This case has been quite difficult to solve. It is a female subject from insular Italy. The extract of her official birth record states birth at 8 pm, while her parents insist it was 5 pm. This may apparently be the typical case in which the parents are wrong, but as I told you – in this case it is not so simple. I ask about the various zodiac signs in the lady's family tree – only a daughter of Cancer and no relative of Leo. Even her diseases seem to express mainly *Cancerine* features, namely a serious problem at the breast and continuous heartburn that required even a gastroscopy. However, the medical examination gave negative results. Saturn on her Descendant could explain a long–running dispute with her brother over a hereditary issue.

To make a long story short, at first sight it seems that in this case the parents' memory is more accurate that the officially recorded time of birth, which is quite unusual. But, as I wrote at the beginning of this section of the book, your interrogation must be done seriously. You have to seek to expose your own false beliefs, those of your counselee, those of his or her relatives – and even those of the official records of birth. In other words, even if you were a Sagittarian supported by an unwavering candour, you should still wear the shoes of Perry Mason and adopt his ways so deeply as to become extremely wary, more suspicious of a double or triple Virgo!

That's exactly what I did in this case. First, I delved into the question of the breast. It turned out that her problem was no disease but only of an aesthetic nature. She had asked a cosmetic surgeon to reshape it in the early nineties. Later on, the prostheses had caused her some difficulties and she faced the alternative of replacement or removal, but in the meantime she had become quite a hypochondriac with fixed ideas of diseases. Hence my first suspect: am I facing with a problem Cancer–breast or Leo–aesthetics?

Once this light switched on in my mind, I went on testing this hypothesis. Meanwhile, I remember that the gastritis is a classic psychosomatic illness that affects almost equally both Cancer and Capricorn. I verified if this lady could have the Ascendant in the sign of Leo.

"Have you ever had small heart problem?"

"Yes, I had a slight tachycardia, but it was just a question of nerves..."

"But is it you who think that you have tachycardia, or has it been diagnosed by the doctor?"

"My doctor has diagnosed it..."

"I see… You see, madam, it is important for me to determine whether something can be classified as *subjective* or *objective*. Regardless of what caused your tachycardia, it is now established that *there is* a tachycardia. And have you ever had problems at your back?"

"Yes, I can not explain it better, but I have an injured or wrong vertebra."

I began to see a little light. At this point, I went on asking many questions with the aim of detecting whether this lady had attempted a career as an artist in the past, or she had ever worked in a movie picture, perhaps as a director, and the like.

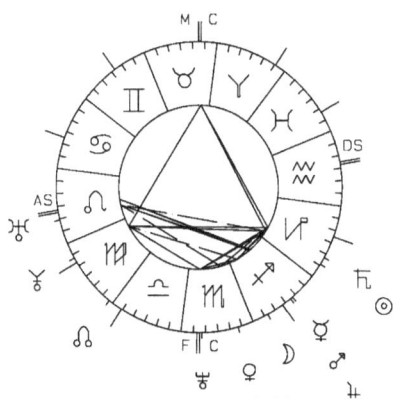

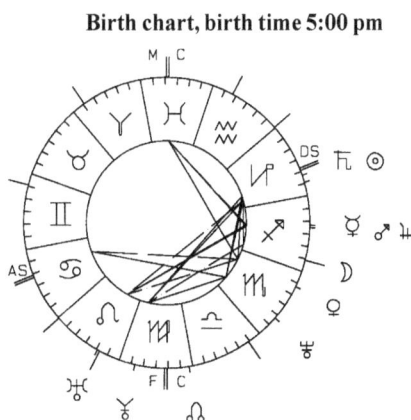

Birth chart, birth time 5:00 pm

Birth chart, birth time 8:00 pm

On this specific field she is quite categorical in saying that hers had always been only feeble inclinations, but that she had never made any practical step to make them real. This left me somewhat puzzled because, after an initial misstep, it seemed that I had chosen the right path. But if you have faith in the stars the stars do not disappoint you. They *never* do it. In fact, refining my questions, I get to know that she has a daughter who is fond of cinema (she is about to sign up for a course in film direction in Rome) and a son who excels in sports.

Now everything matches and I can accept, at least as a first approximation, the officially recorded time of birth.

Case 27

Male subject, from Piedmont, who works in the insurance field. He was born in mid–December but his parents declared him in the following January, indicating 11 o'clock as his time of birth – a completely unreliable time, according to him. In fact, his mother claims to remember his birth very well: it was 5:30 in the morning and 'it was dawning'. I stress that the day he was born the dawn took place at 7:30 am, not at 5:30. He replies that if it is so, then we must make reference to 5:30 am and forget about dawn.

I proceed without any remarks, as is my habit, and start by exploring before anything else the birth chart cast for the officially recorded time of birth (11 o'clock). Actually, this time of birth does not correspond in any way to the man sitting in front of me.

Then I proceed with the time given by his mother (5:30), trying – of course – to verify whether it has been rounded up.

So I ask if there are Scorpios in his family, but he can not remember any solar sign in his family tree. These are our following questions and answers.

"Have you ever suffered from minor problems to the genitals or anus?"

"Never!"

"OK, let's see. Have you ever undergone surgery at your penis or testicles?"

"As a child I had a small operation in my scrotum because of certain veins that had 'fallen down' too much."

"Have you ever had small venereal infections?"

"Never!"

"Not even smaller problems, such as candidiasis or the like, for example?"

"Oh yes, a candidiasis, yes, but it was a woman who infected me *(sic!)*"

"Nothing else?"

"Yes, a fungal disease, other insignificant things..."

"OK, now let's consider your anus. Have you ever suffered from haemorrhoids?"

"Never!"

"Haven't you ever had even the beginnings of haemorrhoids?"

"Yes, yes an initial stage, but they were caused by overeating..."

"Please, let *me* decide whether astrology also has to do with your haemorrhoids or not..."

A long series of questions follow to determine if his natal Sun is in the Second House. His answers are all negative, while he admits a periodic headache that, of course, is consistent with the Sun's position in the First House – not in the second. Furthermore, there is a tremendous bereavement because of a granddaughter who died in a road accident, as well as some legal trouble.

At this point I think that I must stick, for the time being, to a rectified time of birth around 5:10 am, with the man's Ascendant at the end of Scorpio (this does not mean that Scorpio is non–existent in his First House) and with his Sun in the First House.

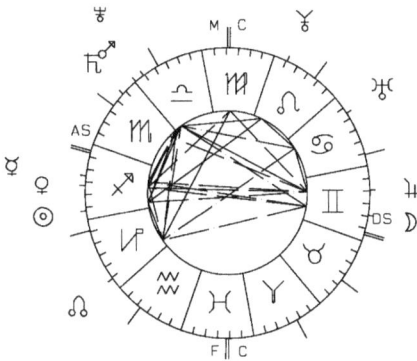

Birth chart, birth time 5:30 am

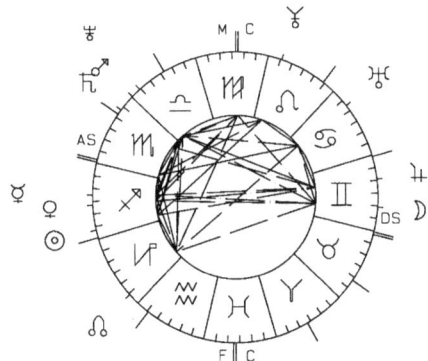

Birth chart, birth time 5:10 am

Case 28

Female subject from northern Italy. She produces *three* different times of birth: 9:30 am (*claiming that her mother remembers it very well...*), 2:30 pm (*claiming that her uncles remember it very well...*) and 11:30 am (*this is the officially recorded time, but she insists that I must ignore it*).

Of course, my questions start considering the latter time of birth: 11:30.

"Is there anybody in your family tree belonging to the sign Pisces?"

"A sister."

I ask the lady to produce the birth dates of her three children and I find that all of them have their natal Moon in Pisces.

"Have you ever suffered any problems at your feet?"

"As a kid I underwent surgery to correct a deformation."

"Nothing else?"

"I often suffer from corns and I hardly bear wearing shoes."

"Can you tell me anything positive about your feet? Perhaps you like dancing?"

"As a child I danced in a school, for three to four years."

"Do you feel a calling to offer nursing assistance to others? If so, can you prove this to me with objective facts of your life?"

"For a couple of decades I assisted my little sister. She had a bad heart disease. I treated her like my own daughter. I used to take her to the doctors, to the hospitals, for check–ups, exams and so on. I cared for her very much."

This answer makes me think that I am on track: her natal conjunction Moon–Venus in Aquarius is not in her Eleventh House but in her Twelfth House (the heart–sick sister).

"Have you or a close family member ever had a severe car accident?"

"One of my brothers was injured seriously enough in the legs."

"Have you ever had trouble from people born in other regions or in a country other than your own?"

"Yes, it has happened to me..."

"Could I describe your mother as a rigid, severe, upright person?"

"Yes, because she had a hard life. She had to bring us up without our father, and she had to take on the stern paternal role."

Obviously with these questions I'm trying to determine if the lady's Saturn is closely conjunct the Medium Coeli.

"Does your mother suffer from any bone disease?"

"Yes, she does."

"Have you or a close family member ever experienced troubles with law?"

"I have: I once underwent an assessment for tax liabilities by the Customs and Excise officers."

At this point I believe that I can have no further doubt. In a provisional, yet quite clearly confirmed way, I decide that this lady's Ascendant lies around 13 to 14 degrees of Pisces, consistent with a time of birth around 11:15.

Birth chart, birth time 2:30 pm

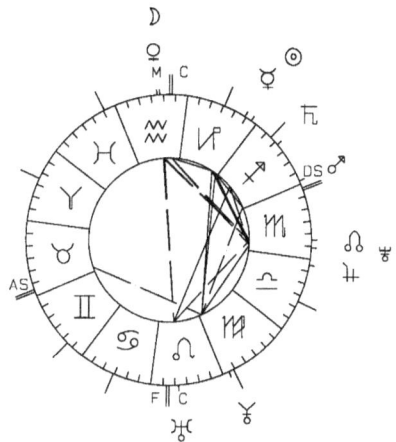

Birth chart, birth time 9:30 am

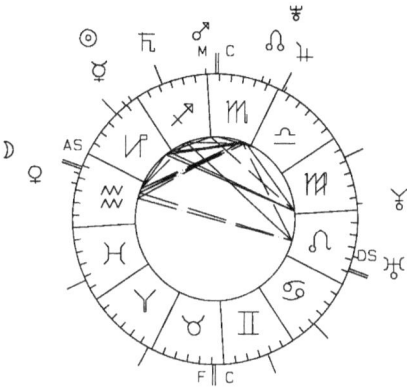

Birth chart, birth time 11:15 am

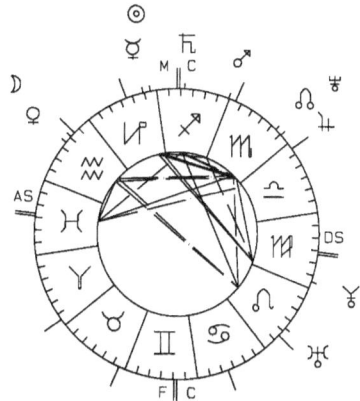

Birth chart, birth time 11:30 am

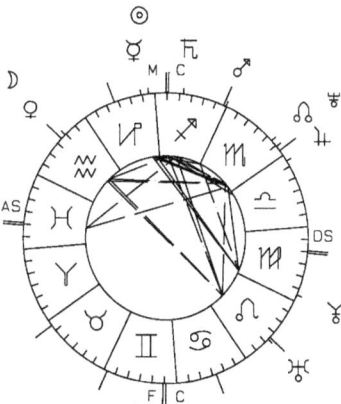

Case 29

Another example of mythologies. Female subject from Apulia, born on the 8th of December. According to the registry she was born at 7:25 but according to her mother (who swears that she remembers it very well!) she was born at 8:30. As you may know the 8th of December is the feast of the Immaculate Conception and, especially in the South of Italy, this occurrence is very heartfelt. For a mother it is nice to be able to boast that she has delivered a pretty cute girlie on the day associated with the Holy Virgin Mary. Yet mythologies are mythologies – you have to be able to support them with some piece of evidence… hence the detailed account of the mother: with a fairly complex series of reconstructions, she can give birth to the child exactly during the passage of the statue of the Virgin Mary or during some other time synchronization with an important moment of that celebration. I just simply can't remember well her words, because to tell you the truth, I do not believe a word of her reconstruction. First of all, I am willing to test the official time of birth (7:25). In fact – I think – if indeed the child had been born at 8:30 why should her parents have to declare '7:25' to the clerk of the registry of births?

My counselee is a tall and slender; she has an imposing, queen–like posture. She is a nice, sunny, radiant woman. She does not wear glasses. All this is surely the expression of a ruling Sun. But as I have said repeatedly, you must be wary of everything, even of your own certainties.

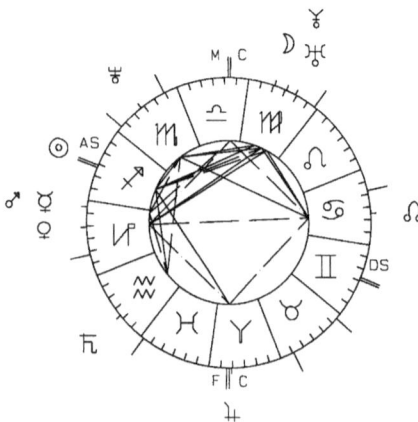

Birth chart, birth time 8:30 am

Birth chart, birth time 7:25 am

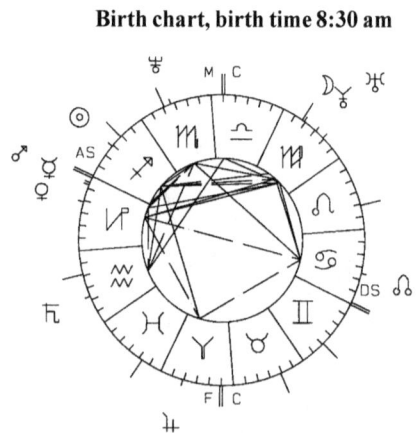

So I proceed with the interrogation. Further questions and answers let me know that the lady has never suffered from anything on the eyes and feet, while she reports she had suffered from sinusitis or some similar headache. Also, she has never had accidental loss or theft of money or similar events. She has never undergone major grief. Finally, she considers herself to be very lucky with the houses she has lived in and/or she has owned.

At this point, I think there can be no doubt that the time closest to the real one is the first: 7:25. I note it down then, on a provisional basis.

Case 30

This is the case of verification rather than rectification. It's a female subject from Abruzzo. Her birth certificate is missing, so I can rely only on her mother's memory, who claims she was born at 10:15 am. First of all I ask her if she has close relatives of Aries.

She tells me that one of her daughters is Aries. Then I ask if she has ever suffered a great loss of money or if she has ever had to fight for an inheritance or a settlement, a bequest, etc. Once again she confirms I am right.

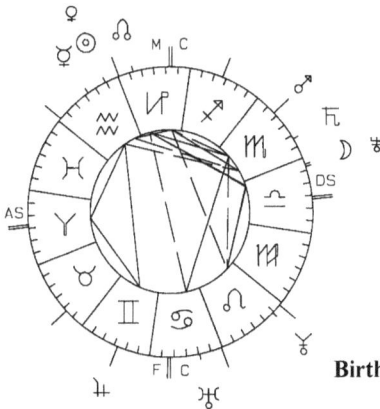

Birth chart, birth time 10:15 am

In fact, after parting from her husband she had disputed the ownership of a house that her husband had originally bought for a child, and had later donated it to her. This caused 14 years of lawsuits, and she eventually had lost it. She also confirms she has strong musical interests and that she suffers from problems of blood circulation (although they would be in any case consistent with the strong elements of Aquarius in her birth chart). She also confirms her passion for driving the car.

On the other hand, for the time being I am not able to establish whether her Uranus lies in the 4th or in the 5th House. In fact, it is true that her house had been suddenly 'snatched' from her, but we can also interpret it in another way – actually it was her son who had been 'severely and suddenly deprived' of the house.

For now I rectify her time to 10 o'clock, pending further investigation.

Case 31

It is a male subject, non Italian. He says that his time of birth is 11:30 pm, of which his parents are 'absolutely sure'.

At a first visual inspection this time seems not to fit, because the man has an intensively pockmarked face – which is very typical of an ascendant Capricorn – but one should never stop at appearances. I ask him if he has close relatives of Sagittarius, and he tells me that his mother was born in early December. I ask him if he has ever suffered from liver disease, and he also confirms it. He says that he is been having rather abnormal transaminase values, for years, without a precise cause.

I ask him if he has ever hurt his legs. Once again his answer is positive: a motorcycle accident caused him a large gash in his leg. At this point I think that his Ascendant must necessarily be in Sagittarius (perhaps it covers a good part of the sign of Capricorn) and that his natal conjunction of Uranus–Pluto must be in the 9th House. I ask some more questions whose answers seem to confirm my assumptions and I provisionally consider his true time of birth to be 11 pm.

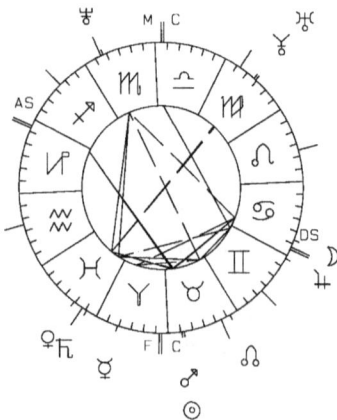

Birth chart, birth time 11:00 pm

Birth chart, birth time 11:30 pm

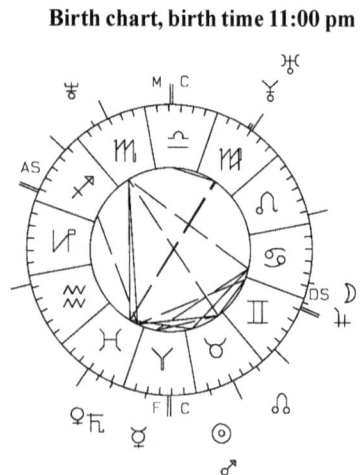

Case 32

A female subject from Veneto. The time is remembered by her parents to be around 8:45 in the morning. My first questions tend to verify her very strong *Piscine* values, which she would have also in the case her Ascendant would be Aquarius (because if so her Sun would be in the Twelfth House). I do not have to work so hard to detect it, because this lady is very smart and she immediately understands what I am trying to do.

As a child (if I remember it correctly) one of her optic nerves was longer that the other. This caused her to be forced to about four years of tough remedial gymnastics. Even today, when she doesn't pay attention, one eye 'goes on its own'. As for the foot, by mere chance she once discovered that she was wearing shoes of a smaller size than her feet, so that her toes became cramped and their skin worn back. She suffered terribly until she started wearing wider shoes. She also has a bunion and, if I am not wrong, she had also suffered a bad fracture in one foot.

Furthermore there is *extremely objective* evidence of a strong vocation or spirit of nursing assistance, proven by years of taking care of different relatives. I can also detect confirmation of her Mars lying in the 2nd House (once all the family jewellery, inherited from her grandmother, was stolen); of her Jupiter in the 7th House (she is having a bad trial of separation from her husband); as well as of many other important elements of her birth sky. However, for a true first amendment I must try to understand whether her natal Saturn is truly in the 9th House or if it must be considered closely conjunct to the MC.

Birth chart, birth time 8:20 am

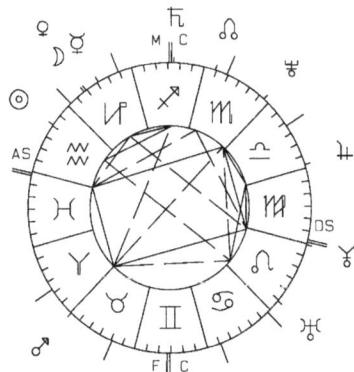

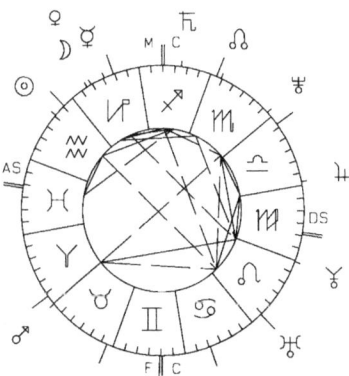

Birth chart, birth time 8:45 am

Hence a long series of questions that make me exclude the first hypothesis and lend support to the latter. Among other things, she and her mother (a severe, moderately cold, serious, earnest woman) have always been distant. Only a few years before her mother died, she experienced a mutual rapprochement.

For these reasons I decide to consider, for the moment, the following time of birth: 8:20.

Case 33

This is a young woman from Calabria with a brilliant career. The time mentioned by her mother is 2:30. She shows very clear values of Gemini – she appears to be very bright, smart, clever, mentally and physically mobile, she always answers very quickly. She smokes enough; she loves reading and studying, as well as driving cars. Despite her young age she is already a manager in a fairly important company. Since the beginning of our conversation I suspect she has also important elements of Taurus, perhaps her Sun is in the 2nd House, not in the 3rd. Therefore many of my questions are aimed to detect the true position of her natal Sun.

"Have you ever suffered in the throat?"

"Never!"

"Have you ever had your tonsils removed?"

"Ah, oh, well, yeah, that's obvious…"

"I do not think it is… Can I say that you often experience spans of time in which you feel some sort of discomfort with food? For example, have you ever had lighter forms of anorexia or bulimia?"

"Yes, I have – quite frequently."

"Have you ever had a thyroid investigation?"

"I'm going to have them done, since my excessive thinness can not be explained otherwise."

"As you can see, maybe throat has something to do with you… Do smells stir in you a particular attention, either in a positive or a negative way?"

Both she and her boyfriend clearly confirm.

"Do you like the countryside?"

"Yes, I like it very much."

"Can you tell me something positive, referring to the throat? Do you like singing? Have you ever tried? Are you fond of singing or music?"

"My mother is an opera singer. I tried to take singing lessons, but then I stopped. I simply *adore* listening to people singing and playing."

In addition to all this, take into consideration that her father is Taurus.

Several other questions followed that would confirm an earlier time, perhaps advanced of only one quarter of an hour – still, enough to place her natal Sun within the orb of two and a half degrees from the cusp between the 2nd and the 3rd House. For the time being I leave it at that and I invite the lady to produce her birth certificate.

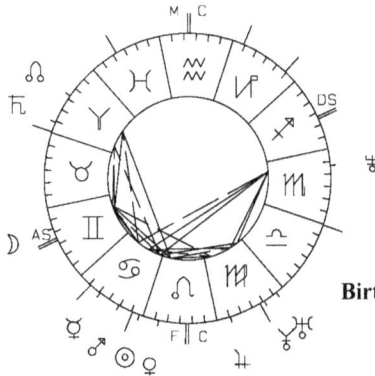

Birth chart, birth time 2:30 am

Case 34

It is a female subject born in Sardinia. Her mother (mummy is always right...) declares that she was born at 10:30. However the officially recorded time of birth is eight o'clock in the morning.

"Have you relatives of Libra?"

"Yes, one of my sons."

"Have you ever undergone surgery?"

"Never!"

"Are you sure? Just think about it. If you set me on the wrong track it is to your disadvantage."

"Well, now that I remember… I had a Caesarean section. And also a plastic surgery at my breast, but it was me who decided in the latter case!"

"Any abortion?"

"Yes, I had four."

"So it is six operations so far. Are you forgetting anything else?"

"No."

"Let's talk about your feet now. Have you a bunion?"

"Do you mean the big toe? Yes, it hurts me very badly but I decided not to undergo surgery because I am told that the operation can be very painful."

"Are you flat–footed?"

"A little.

"Do you walk in a 'strange' way?"

"So they say."

"Have you ever had ingrown toenails?"

Now read this answer carefully: it is very nice and very original.

"Yes, from time to time I have. But it's as if I had not because I solve everything at the beautician, without going to the doctor."

"Do you recognize you have a spirit of nursing / caring assistance?"

"Not at all."

"But have you ever assisted somebody, perhaps for long periods, providing care even if unwillingly?"

"Yes, my husband, for example."

At this point I ask other questions whose answers confirm, without a doubt, that this lady's birth took place at least a quarter of an hour or half an hour earlier that 8 o'clock, the officially recorded time.

With further questions I can also detect that, virtually at one hundred percent, her natal Saturn falls in the 3rd House and not in the 4th. But I need a litmus test to determine whether her time of birth is closer to 7:30 or to 7:45. So I correct her last Solar Return for the earlier time of birth and I see a very bad stellium in the 7th House, which usually heralds conflicts, officially stamped paper, troubles with bureaucracy, with the law or anything like that. But if the lady reported she had a love affair instead, then her Saturn would surely be in the 5th House.

"With whom have you been fighting for the last months?"

"With my husband. Mind you: the very day of my birthday I discovered he had another woman!

For the time being I think that the most likely time of birth is 7:30.

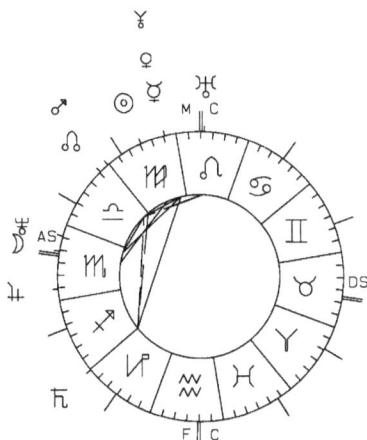

Birth chart, birth time 8:00 am

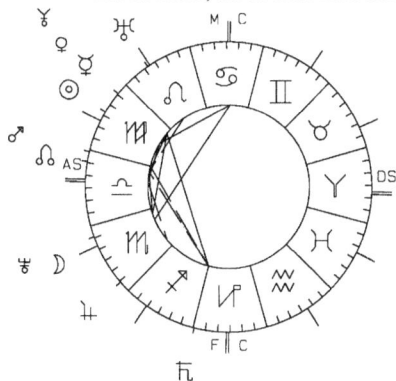

Birth chart, birth time 10:30 am

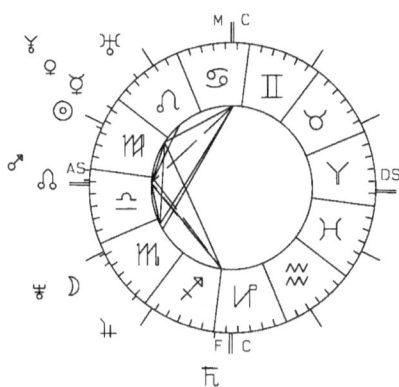

Birth chart, birth time 7:30 am

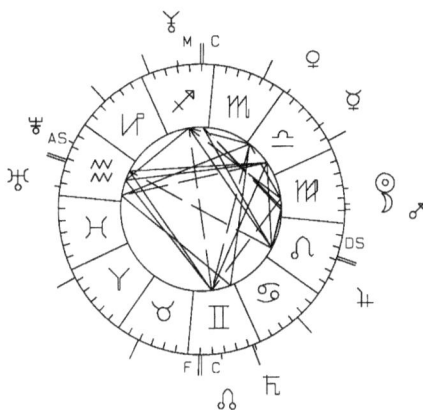

SR if the time of birth is 7:30 am

Case 35

This is a male from Friuli, a teacher in a high school. Based on the memories of his parents, he claims he was born at 10 o'clock. He does not have any brothers or sisters: he is unmarried; he has no children; he has very few relatives; he hardly remember his parents' solar sign – hence, in this case astral heredity can not help me at all.

"Do you like music or singing very much?"

"I love music; I would be listening to music constantly."

"Have you ever had problems with blood circulation?"

"Yes, in one of my eyes. I'm under medical control for that."

"Have you ever had trouble with your hearing?"

"Healing?"

"No, not healing – *hearing*."

"Ah, here, so – well, in fact, as you can see I am a little bit deaf."

Many more questions follow that determine, without fear of contradiction, that his natal stellium is in the Eleventh House and that his natal Mars is in the Third House. Therefore I consider, as a first approximation, that his time of birth is 9:30.

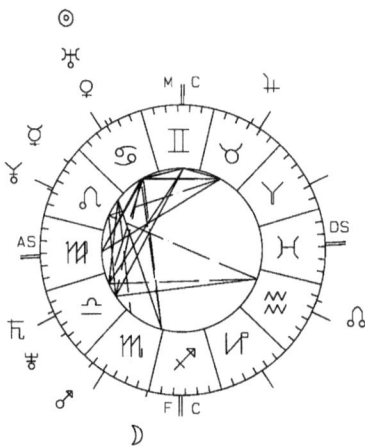

Birth chart, birth time 10:00 am

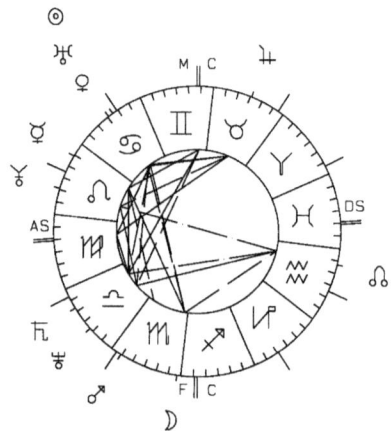

Birth chart, birth time 9:30 am

Case 36

A male subject from Rome, whose work is to do with the arts. His mother 'swears' that he was born at 10:10 pm, but I see that he has a very *Scorpionic* and little *Sagittarian* appearance. Unluckily, he has very few relatives, whose dates of birth fade in the native's little bit obscured memories.

But he has a daughter. I ask for her birth data and I cast her chart: Ascendant in Scorpio and extremely strong elements in the Eighth House.

So I ask, "Have you ever suffered from haemorrhoids?"

"Yes, often."

I ask many other questions that confirm what now appears quite evident:

his Ascendant is Scorpio and so, for now, I moved back his time of birth by some twenty minutes.

Birth chart, birth time 10:10 pm

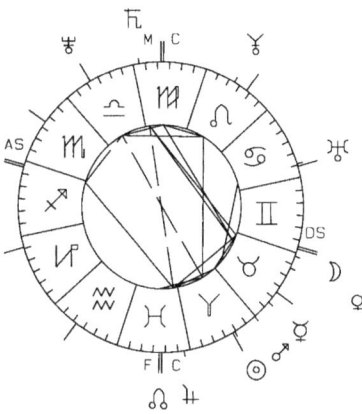

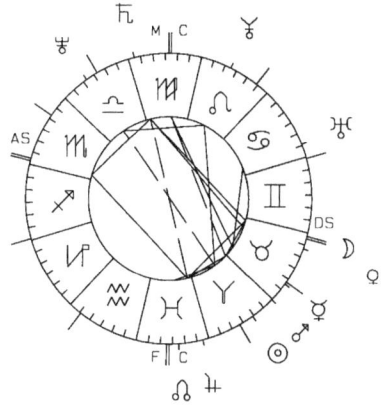

Birth chart, birth time 9:50 pm

Case 37

This is a male subject from southern Lazio. The extract of his birth record states 0:35 am. I present this case as an example, and it is not the only one, to demonstrate once again that the 'prejudice' that must accompany your questioning should cover 360 degrees – thus distrusting your own prejudice. If the facts show that the native is right, then you will certainly *give to Caesar what is Caesar's*. His parents fully agree with the officially recorded time of birth. His mother, being fond of astrology, was very careful to time the event. The only real doubt that I could consider is the position of his natal Sun: if the time is correct, it is in the Third House.

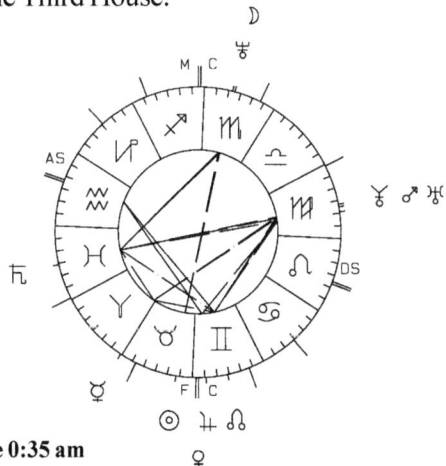

Birth chart, birth time 0:35 am

But if I was facing the usual rounding up of the official time, his natal Sun could be in the Fourth House instead. The facts ascertained during the interview give reason to the extract of the birth record, as well as to the native's parents. In fact, his wife's brother used to suffer from serious problems of depression and eventually committed suicide.

His wife became a victim of an armed robbery in her own shop. The native himself has two pending criminal charges, for really minor, silly behaviour. The aforementioned brother–in–law was very much present in the life of this man, who had to take care of him for many years before his death.

A long series of other questions confirm the given time. Maybe it's not 0:35, but at most it could be 0:25 and in this case I prefer to leave the official time unchanged.

Case 38

This is a female subject born in Calabria, who lives in Veneto. The time stated in her birth record is 4 pm. It is the same time remembered by her parents, but it is not credible at all – for the reasons that you will see now. This woman is unmarried and without children. She moved to the north of Italy when she was no loner young. She tried to get a job to do with the arts, but ten years after she is only struggling through, economically speaking, rather than making a living. I could say that from a professional point of view, hers has been an almost total failure.

She confirms that she has dental troubles (she has always had) and also problems at her knees. She also confirms a number of problems with the law, though not serious ones. Now, if I accepted that she was born at 4 o'clock I would be faced with a case without any astrological explication. Should I use astrological evidence to demonstrate the validity of astrology to its detractors, I would surely use the example of a birth chart in which Jupiter lies in the Sixth House, which in the overwhelming majority of cases corresponds to people who are easily able to succeed in their work.

But this seems to be exactly the opposite case. So I try downgrading her time by thirty minutes and reconsidering everything. Having rectified her time of birth this way, it seems to me that things can now be explained quite well. Jupiter is in her 7th House and not in the 6th. This is why it could not help her at all at work. Venus and Saturn become ruling planets in the MC, in Gauquelin sector (where you can also accept a large conjunction with an orb of almost ten degrees). The ruling Venus indicates the artistic vocation of her profession. The ruling Saturn explains her lack of success, especially clearly if you consider that she was trying to establish a professional reputation for herself in a 'foreign land'. Let me stress that if there is a close conjunction Venus–Saturn in the vicinity of the MC, in Gauquelin sector, the result is always that of a Saturn that clearly prevails over Venus.

For now I leave her birth time rectified to 3:30 pm. Of course, before deciding so I directed many more questions at this lady, but I don't list them simply because I don't want to overburden this paragraph.

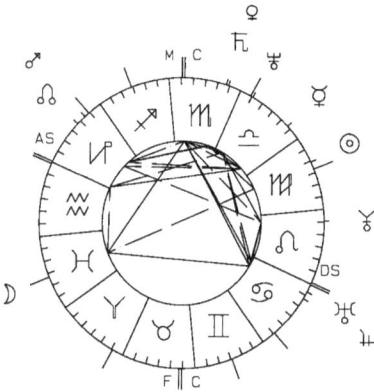

Birth chart, birth time 4:00 pm

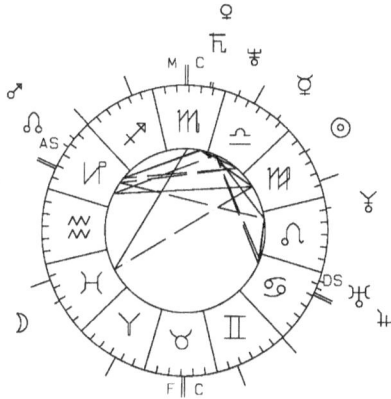

Birth chart, birth time 3:30 pm

Case 39

Even in this case, the time may be precise or perhaps only slightly rounded up. This is a young man and in the last couple of decades the general interest in astrology has increased so that even the staffs of the delivery room are more careful to record the exact times of birth of the babies.

And he could also produce a birth certificate that matches the memory of his parents: both sources state 10:10 am. This is a tall, good looking boy who studies languages. He once suffered a fairly serious car accident, but without injury. He has practiced many sports. He has a sister whom he defines 'a little original'. He is good at doing many different things with hands, massage among them.

And he certainly is more Aquarius than Cancer – he is very outgoing, he would like to work in the field of public relations, he loves music, and friendship is extremely important to him. Therefore, for the time being I leave his time of birth unchanged.

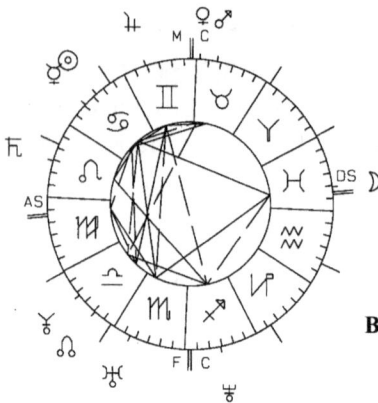

Birth chart, birth time 10:10 am

Case 40

This is really a very peculiar case, which allows you to probe a little further into the mechanisms of psychological repression, or in the difficulties of communication between the counselee and the astrologer. This is a woman from Emilia–Romagna, claiming that her time of birth is 6:15 pm according to her parents' memory.

Obviously my attention is immediately captured by her very ugly conjunction Mars–Saturn very close to the cusp between the 4th and the 5th House. My first attempt is consequently to discover if this conjunction actually lies in the 5th House –which appears quite likely. I must be very careful, though, and proceed with caution. In fact, there could be a big problem involved with this celestial position. So I have to treat her with 'mental' kid gloves using all the worldly wisdom that psychology makes available to man.

"Do you have children?"

"One."

"You have one. Is it because you have decided so, or is it because life hasn't given you more?"

"No, we had one and we have not longed for having more. Why do you ask me?" – questions the lady with concern – "Do you see anything bad concerning my son?"

"No, no, please be reassured. I am just asking questions to try to correct your time of birth. Has your child ever caused problems of any kind?"

"No, not at all."

So I go on asking indirect or *oblique* questions, but it is quite clear to me that her answers are not convincing at all, although I can not say it openly to her. So I try to ask further questions searching for other elements that may give evidence of the presence of this detrimental conjunction in her natal 5th House. I am able to do so without making her understand my goal, also because this lady does not deal with astrology and knows nothing of its symbols.

"Have you ever had serious troubles with your heart or genitals?"

"No, never."

"Have you ever had abortions?"

"No, never."

"Have you ever suffered severe disappointments in love?"

"I am separating from my husband, but I can not say that this makes me tear my hair out in despair."

"You are a teacher. Has there ever been uncomfortable happenings with the students you have to deal with?"

"Well, yes. Last year a colleague of mine was accused to have molested a boy and I was the person in charge for the school then." – *At least this is what I have understood from her answer.* – "However I was not directly involved."

"And you, personally, as a child, have you ever experienced traumas related to attempted sexual assaults or lesser sexual harassment?"

"Yes, but they were little things."

Personally up to that point the story did not convince me at all and I thought, "There are only two possibilities: either this woman is blocked by a mechanism or psychological repression, or her real time of birth is totally far from the given one."

In similar cases, as I have already explained, my 'technique' within the interrogation is to change the topic completely to allow the counselee to feel at ease, to relax, to leave a position of contracture in her or his posture, and above all – to talk as much as possible. This is what I did: you shall see what incredible story came out.

When she was twenty years old, the lady was told that she could never have children, except in case of 'a miracle'. To tell the truth, she did not suffer at all from this diagnosis; actually she did not care that much.

Once again, the astrological symbolism is clear and even redundant. It explains that the touch of cynicism connected with her natal conjunction Mars–Saturn had actually found its practical expression either in love or with children. Obviously, given the facts that I am exposing, I am not just talking about the fairly cynical attitude of this lady – I am rather talking about the general halo of gravity that this dangerous conjunction in her natal 5th House has carried to her existence.

Birth chart, birth time 6:15 pm

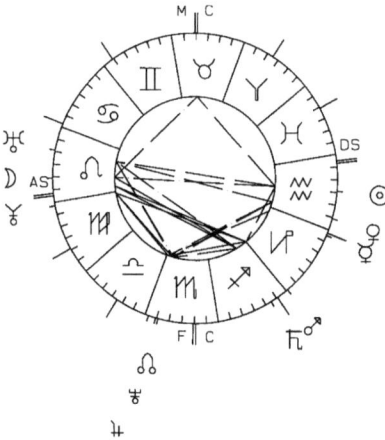

Birth chart, birth time 6:00 pm

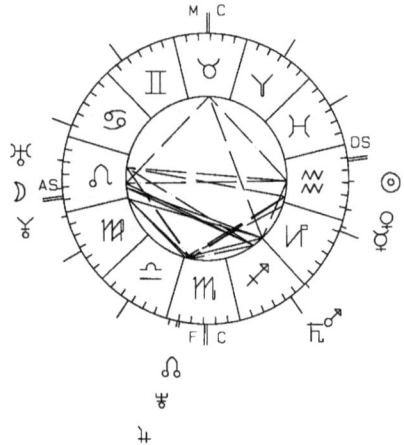

Twelve years later (Saturn in the fifth acting as Kronos, the old age, the delay) the 'miracle' happened and she became pregnant – a news for which she was not glowing with happiness though. Currently, her child has some quite serious forms of allergy, with considerable problems involving breathing (still connected with the mother's bad conjunction Mars–Saturn in the Fifth House).

This is all – and I believe it should be sufficient and it is even more than enough.

On the basis of many other questions and answers I temporarily consider a rectified time of birth of 6 pm.

Case 41

Female subject born in Campania, who lives in Lazio. Her mother is sure that she was born at 9 pm, but at first glance I suspect that her natal Sun may be in the 6th House and not in the 5th. Therefore I ask some questions aimed to detect this detail.

"Have you close relatives of Scorpio?"

"My mother and my sister."

"Have you ever suffered, in the past, due to gynaecological problems or haemorrhoids?"

"Haemorrhoids, yes."

"Have you good manual skills? What can you do well, with your hands?"

"I used to enjoy – and I still like – knitting, crocheting, embroidering..."

"Do you like sending or receiving massages?"

"Both things."

"Have you ever tried playing the piano or the guitar?"

"The guitar."

"What do you do?"

"I am a designer."

"(!)"

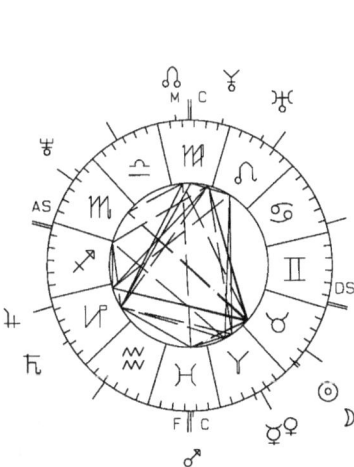

Birth chart, birth time 8:30 pm

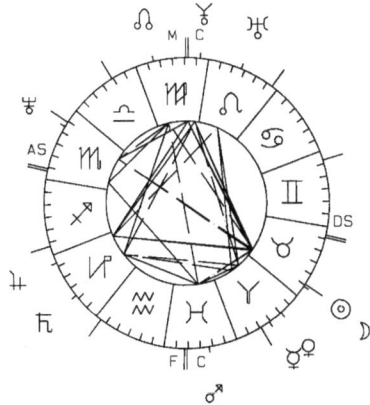

Birth chart, birth time 9:00 pm

Many other questions follow. From the lady's answers it also turns out that, at the age of forty–three years, she has never been married despite having had many love affairs.

I provisionally consider a time of birth of 8:30 pm.

Case 42

Female subject from Tuscany. Her mother says she was born at 0:15, while the officially recorded time is 12 o'clock. In these cases (I mean, when the time of birth is around noon or midnight) it is very easy to determine which of the two times is true, even though rounded up or down.

Generally speaking, as you may have guessed, I doubt the statements of the parents and I consider that the statements of the birth record are more reliable. In this case it would be even more difficult to understand why the lady's father or any other relative, the day after her birth, would have chosen to declare 12 o'clock instead of 0:15 – while I really can not imagine any logical path that could have led them to take the opposite decision (thus declaring 0:15 if the birth had really taken place at midnight).

However, as I always said, during the *interview* I tend to be suspicious of everything, especially of my own beliefs. Therefore I proceed without prejudice – or better said: *with all the necessary prejudices*.

"Have you relatives of Pisces, Virgo, or Capricorn?"

"One of my parents is Pisces. Also one of my daughters is a Pisces. One of my sisters is Capricorn."

It should be noted that if she were born at 12 o'clock, the values of the Moon Capricorn would disappear from her birth chart.

"Please list the other signs of your family tree."

She remembers some of them, and I notice that Cancer is repeated several times.

"Do you recognize you have an attitude of nursing and/or caring assistance?"

"No."

Nonetheless after a couple of questions it turns out that during a quite long period she had assisted a terminally ill nun – in the nunnery, not in hospital. I also get to know that she is a special education teacher and that for several years she has been engaging in a spiritual path.

"Let me ask something about your feet. Have you ever had troubles in that part of your body?"

"No, never."

"OK, let's see. Have you a bunion?"

"A little, you can say."

"Maybe you have had, in the past, ingrown toenails?"

"Almost, we can say. What I mean is that there's almost a level of pathology in my nails that may require surgery, but then I can always save them in time."

"Have you ever had a fracture or a burn or an injury to your feet?"

"Only once."

"Could I say that you walk in a somewhat strange fashion?"

"Yes, you could say so."

"Can I say that you need special shoes?"

The lady raises one leg above the height of the desk to show me she is wearing ski boots. She explains that if she wears anything other than this, her feet hurt very badly.

"Excuse me, but for me this is enough trouble at your feet, isn't it? Let's consider your eyes now. Hasn't your mother ever told you that in your childhood you had a slight squi… ?"

"A light squint! Ah! Now you see me normal, but every so often one of my eyes goes one way and the other one goes the other way…"

Exploring the planet *man* is extremely fascinating. After her repeated and surprising omission of foot problems, I would have expect this lady opposing a sort of 'code of silence' when talking of her eyes – for the eyes should be much more important in the vanity of a still attractive woman. On the contrary, she immediately and openly admitted having problems with her eyes.

Other questions and answers make me know that this lady is separated and that her husband is a great neurotic (her Saturn and Neptune are in the Seventh House). Also I hear, after direct questions to which she first replied negatively and then positively, that she has lost a home because of her own naïveté about her husband (Mars in the Eighth House). She has two sons – both came suddenly and unexpectedly (Uranus in the Fifth House).

It is quite clear, at this point, that her time of birth is very close to midnight – but is her Sun lying in the 3rd or in the 4th natal House? Well, first of all, she has several close relatives of Cancer, but it's the following conversation that helps me take the bull by the horns.

"At night, do you prefer to go out or stay home? Let me put in a clearer way. Throughout your life, have you gone out in the evening often, or have you stayed almost always at home?"

"I stayed… I still have been spending much time at home."

For the time being I fixed her time of birth at midnight.

When the lady leaves, she says she's moved and asks for permission to kiss me (on my cheek).

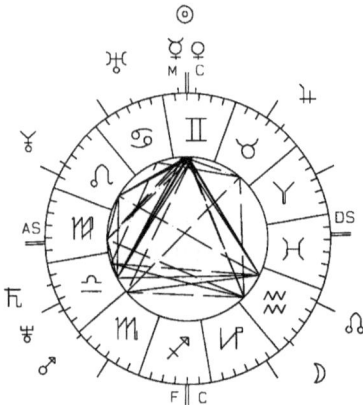

Birth chart, birth time 12:00 am

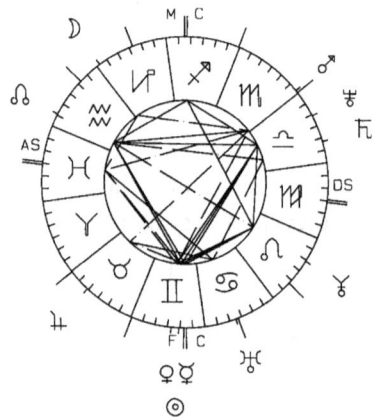

Birth chart, birth time 0:15 am

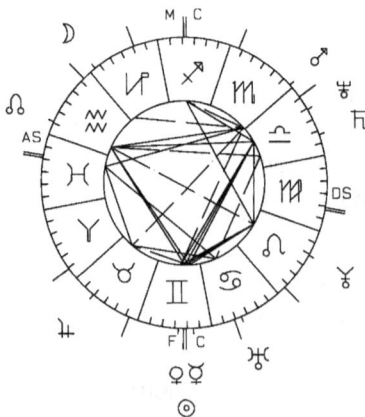

Birth chart, birth time 0:00 am

Case 43

This case is rather more abnormal than normal. It is an attractive girl with big dark eyes, a bit overweight. She arrives with her grandmother who remembers very well that it was 7 in the morning when her granddaughter saw the light for the first time. The document set out in the clinic states it was 7:40. As I have already said many times, times of birth are usually rounded up. But this is the case of a girl born in a major hospital seventeen years ago, and it is quite unlikely that the time marked in the hospital register could be 40 minutes later than the actual time of birth.

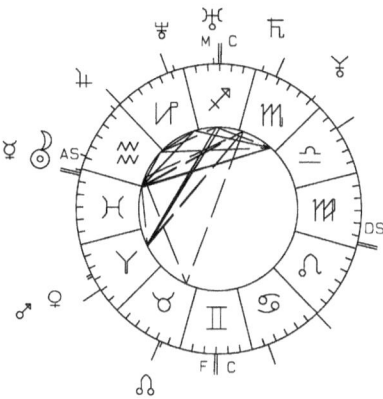

Birth chart, birth time 7:00 am

Birth chart, birth time 7:40 am

Birth chart, birth time 7:20 am

Therefore I ask her several questions starting from this first logical consideration. A preliminary 'watershed' is the position of Saturn in her birth chart. Her father abandoned her and her mother when she was a child. He fled abroad without giving any news of himself thereafter. There can be absolutely no doubt that her Saturn is in the 9th House (not in the 8th), therefore she can not be born *after* 7:20. On the other hand – for a variety of other reasons – she should not be born *before* 7:20 either. If she were, her Jupiter would not be lying in her natal 11th House, while it is clear to me that her Jupiter *is* in the 11th House, having given patent signs of its presence there in the girl's life up to date. So, temporarily, I fix the rectified time at 7:20.

I wish to share with my readers a really interesting detail about this girl. From the very beginning of our meeting, I insist that in my opinion she should attend courses on *shiatsu* and *reiki*. I also warn her to leave out, in the strongest terms, her project to go to Milan (her Saturn is in the 9th House) to study at Bocconi University (there is nothing in her birth chart justifying such a choice).

Both the girl and her grandmother are very surprised by my advice. Then, when taking leave, her grandmother asks me, "Do you know what my niece likes to do the most?"

"No, I don't. What does she?"

"Massages."

Case 44

Male subject from insular Italy. His mother is certain that he was born at 3:30 pm and he does not understand why his time of birth should be different. He is an only child, unmarried and without children. He can not remember the birthdays of his uncles or grandparents. Luckily, he remembers he had been operated for haemorrhoids. He also claims to have suffered from other problems that can be related to the sign of Scorpio.

He also reports a long love affair with an artist. He also reports to have won – quite easily in fact – a long court case connected with car insurance.

All this (together with other elements) makes me almost certain that his natal Venus should be rested in the Seventh House or very close to his Descendant. What is left is determining whether his Mars is actually in the 4th or in the 5th House, considering that his father is Aries and has undergone many operations throughout his life. I would say, of course, that his Mars is in the 4th House and therefore I provisionally leave his time of birth set at 3:10 pm.

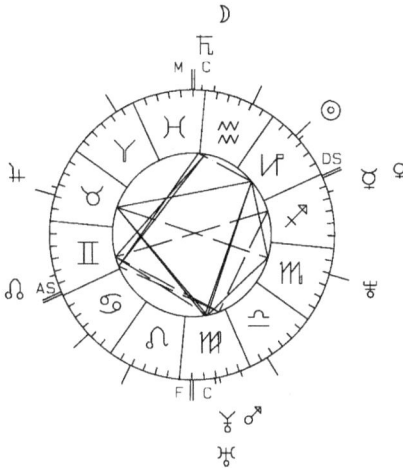

Birth chart, birth time 3:10 pm

Birth chart, birth time 3:30 pm

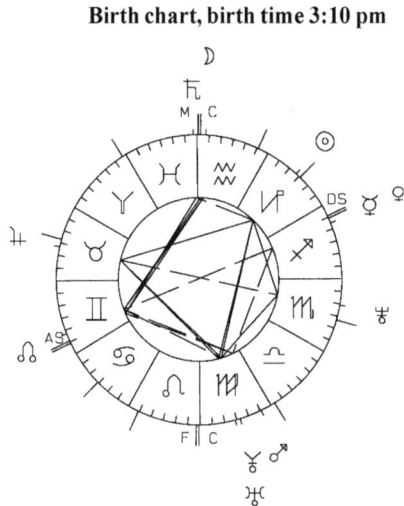

Case 45

The birth record states this person was born at 3:40 am, but the mother remembers it was 3:40 pm. The subject has a son with the Ascendant, plus three celestials, in Cancer. In addition, he is a keen musician (stellium in the 11th House), had a serious problem that led to eye surgery (Mars in the 6th House), and has the typical look of being a bit of a helpless Cancerian, and also protruding belly. He suffers from constipation (which is typical of both Virgo and Cancer). His father used to be treated with electroshocks because of some war trauma; He also suffered from financial troubles for all his life. At this point, which astrologer would ever trust this man's birth certificate?

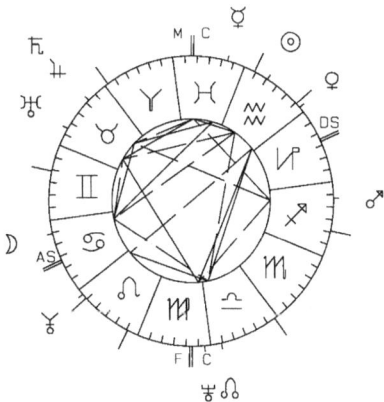

Birth chart, birth time 3:40 am

Birth chart, birth time 3:40 pm

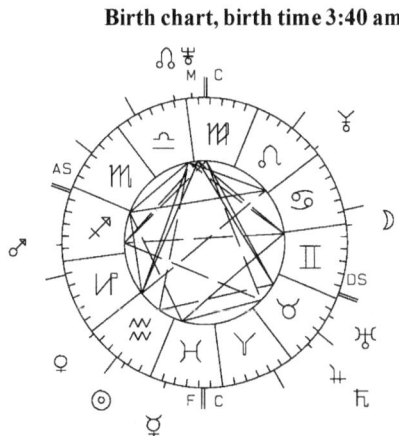

Case 46

Female subject from northern Italy. She is a good locking graduate with clear eyes and an excessive thinness. The extract of her birth certificate states that she was born at 5:30 am – which is confirmed by her parents. All matches pretty well and I would have left this time unchanged, or at most I would have rounded it down by the usual fifteen minutes – but I had a moment of hesitation when I heard that many years before this lady had suffered from severe anorexia, which she was able to overcome with her own strength of will.

I would be tempted, then, to evaluate the possibility of her natal Sun lying in the 2nd House, but this can not be possible, for a few compelling reasons. First, it is highly unlikely that the memory of the parents and the time stated in the birth certificate differ significantly from the actual time of birth. Secondly, there is a brother whose natal chart shows evident elements of Aries. Thirdly, this lady has suffered from sinusitis and, finally, she stands fair chances to have the ruling conjunction of Venus and Mercury right on her Ascendant – apart from her pleasant appearance, this would explain her ability to joke jokes and being so funny...

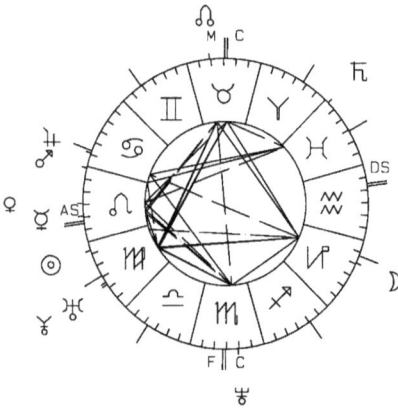

Birth chart, birth time 5:30 am

Case 47

What follows is probably the most difficult case that I have ever faced – and in fact, I don't think I have solved it, for the time being. It's a female subject from Lazio. She is a young friendly woman, dynamic, self–confident, tanned, wearing casuals. My first impulse would be to remove only about fifteen minutes from her officially recorded time of birth: 2:30 pm, which is also confirmed by her parents. In fact, she has the mother, a brother and a sister of Gemini. She had a long love affair with a handsome man, aesthetically speaking. She also experienced a sort of small but almost miraculous rescue in a legal dispute (all this suggesting that her natal Venus is on the Descendant or in the 7th House).

However, there are elements that would suggest –almost mandatorily – that her Sun is in the Ninth House, not in the Eighth. For example she is a very outgoing, open, cheerful individual. She used to practice many sports and even horse riding. She reports that from her very first mount she had the impression of having always been able to go on horseback. She loves animals, travels, and is attracted by everything that comes from abroad. Within few weeks on a Caribbean island, she had almost learned to speak Spanish. Furthermore (!), she has also two brothers of Sagittarius.

However, to consider this assumption valid, I should move back the clock of her birth by nearly an hour – which seems like too much. So, for now, I move back the clock and then I suggest you to relocate her next Solar Return as shown in option B. In fact, in this case, if she were born approximately an hour earlier, in the twelve months covered by this SR she would not have experienced the little 'threat' that Saturn in the Eighth House of SR would certainly be for her if she were born less than an hour earlier, thus falling in the 9th House of SR but at a smaller distance than 2 and a half degrees from the cusp between the 8th and the 9th House.

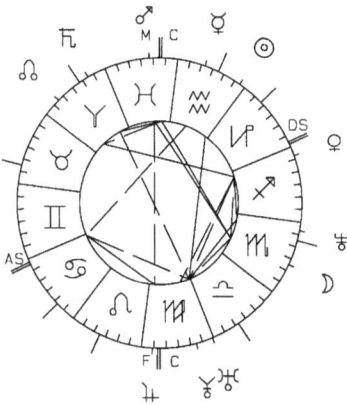

Birth chart, birth time 2:30 pm

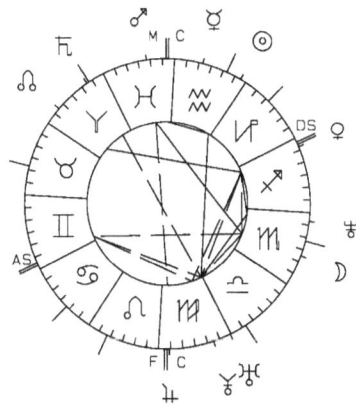

Birth chart, birth time 2:15 pm

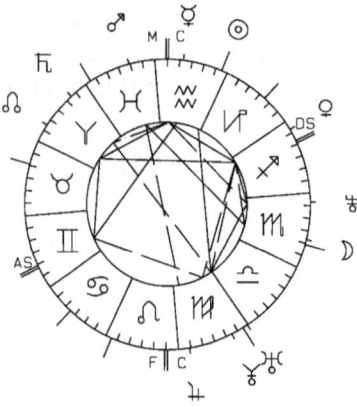

Birth chart, birth time 1:45 pm

Solar Return option A

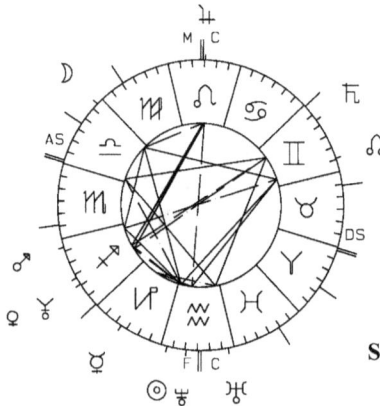

Solar Return option B

Case 48

Perhaps, this case may explain why an astrologer should not try to rectify a time of birth based only on the counselee's photograph. In fact, as an expert astrologer you need to observe your counselee with every sense, in order to study his or her behavioural dynamics. Furthermore you cannot forget, as I mentioned in another section of this book, to notice the counselee's reaction time to your questions, as well as other details such as how his or her skin changes colour depending on the subjects you are facing; how his breathing varies; the calmness or the agitation with which he or she reacts to the questioning, and so on.

This female subject, born in Lombardy, fetched a birth certificate stating that she was born at 4:15 while her mother claimed to remember exactly to the minute (!) that it was 11 pm. But from my very first questions I realized that the real time of birth was very far from her mother's memories. Everything suggested that her birth certificate was absolutely right. This lady in fact had remarkable (and quite unpleasant) skin perspiration. She is a rather stocky woman with a massive neck; her movements are slow and a bit heavy. Add to this that she dearly loves to cook, that she has always suffered from problems related with the throat, and that she used to be a theatre actress for several years in a row (!), I think there can not be other doubts.

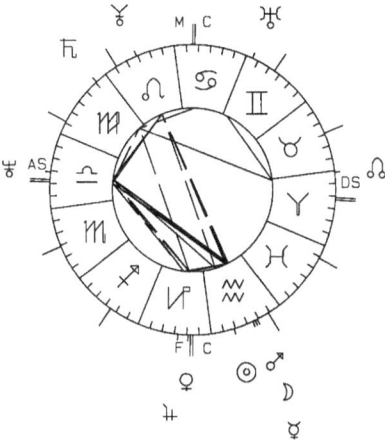

Birth chart, birth time 11:00 pm

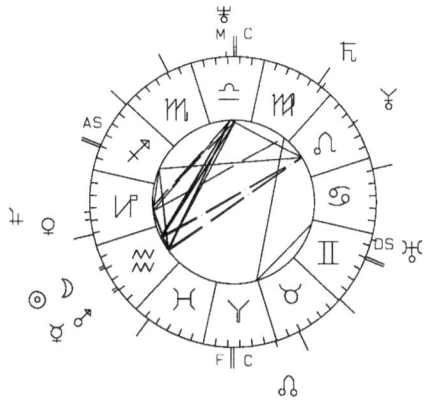

Birth chart, birth time 4:15 am

Case 49

This is a doubtful case. Whoever said that all cases can be solved with the 'interrogation' or with the 'first interview'? This male subject is Sicilian. He tells me that he was born twenty minutes after the beginning of the 17th of November, but his father – who was quite superstitious – resolved to declare that his son was 'actually' born on the 16th. It seems that all the members of his family agree on this point. Now, some events of his life are quite consistent with the given time of birth. For example, one of his grandfathers – who played an important role in his life – was born with the Sun in Virgo. My counselee has also a job that is consistent with this Ascendant. He reports that he has always been suffering at the gastrointestinal system. He also reports a long sequel of interests and hobbies clearly related with a Sun in the 3rd House, and so on. Nonetheless, the following three elements make me doubt, namely: 1) he has undergone surgery only once in his life and it was not for a serious problem; 2) his love life was a disaster;

and 3) he has two daughters with whom he is unable to get along well. Conversely, it should be noted that his two daughters are excellent at their studies and are likely to play a 'special' role in his life.

I do not feel like making dogmatic judgments only on the basis of this conflicting data. Thus, I decide to investigate further. First of all I ask him to produce the copy of his birth record (which I would like to see with my own eyes) and then I ask for the testimony of his aunts still living, and so on.

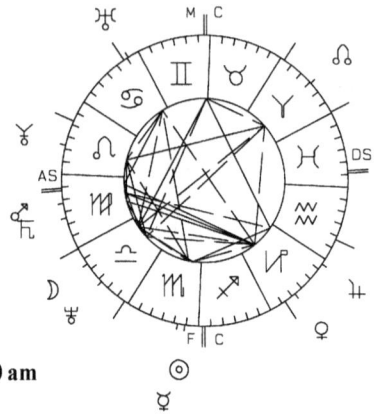

Birth chart, birth time 0:20 am

Case 50

This is a male subject from Rome. He who works in the field of arts, with some success. Both his birth certificate and his mother state that he was born at 6.30 pm, but I do not think so.

He immediately reports that his father was born with the Sun in Pisces, which directs all my subsequent questions. His answers give me a good degree of confirmation.

He is cross–eyed, highly myopic and reports that he slightly suffers at his feet. According to the rule of the *two and a half degrees of distance from a cusp* we must consider that his Sun is acting both in his 7th House and in his 6th House. In fact, as a boy, he had already a clear idea of his own professional future – he would be a lawyer or a judge. Furthermore he also takes a somewhat manic care of his own physical appearance. His father committed suicide when he was a young man.

This would explain very well his conjunction Venus–Neptune in the 8th House, marking his entire life. Some might argue that a Mars in the 4th House could also be a probable indicator of a father dying a violent death

But if so, Mars would be taken away from the cusp of the 5ᵗʰ House, while it is exactly this position that plays a role of key importance in the life of this man. In fact, he has strong interests in the arts (basically, this is his career) and a son showing clear inclinations in the sports.

So, for now, I temporarily subtract one quarter of an hour to the given time (6:30), but those 'little' fifteen minutes really explain a lot of things...

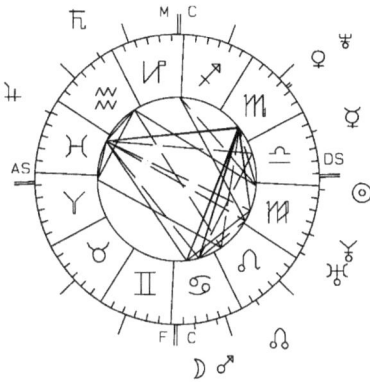

Birth chart, birth time 6:30 pm

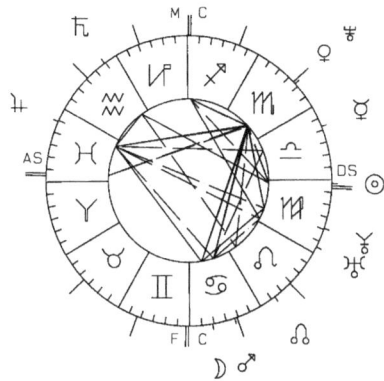

Birth chart, birth time 6:15 pm

Case 51

This is a male subject from the area of Treviso. He does not arrive personally – his wife arrives instead and speaks for him. Both his birth record and his parents agree that he was born at 4:30 pm. I can not have any doubt about his natal Sun lying in the 7ᵗʰ House, because he had several troubles with the law. As a young man, he used to be an extra–parliamentary political activist who gave and received many punches.

He becomes extremely agitated when talking about issues of justice, and when I describe him to his wife as a man living *with the knife in his mouth*, she heartily agrees. However, at this point I try to find out if his Sun can also have some relationships with the Eighth House. In fact, despite being still quite young, this man has prostate problems. Furthermore – and here I would like to put ten exclamation points – having done several jobs in his life, for a certain period he had also assisted a pathologist coroner in over a hundred autopsies. Finally, as a former heart attack patient he has a great and constant fear of dying.

Based on this factual information I decide, for now, to move back his time of birth by half an hour, thus placing his Sun on the cusp between the Seventh and the Eighth House.

Birth chart, birth time 4:30 pm

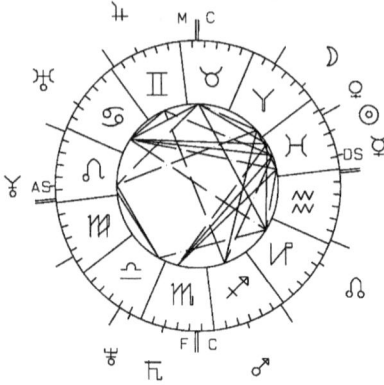

Birth chart, birth time 4:00 pm

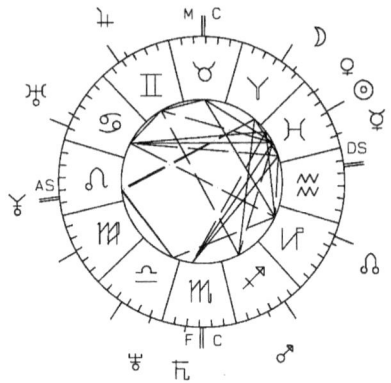

Case 52

This is a fairly easy, yet quite 'striking' case of rectification of the time of birth. It is a female subject from Emilia–Romagna. Both her birth record and the memories of her parents agree on her time of birth being 8:20 in the morning. But my guess is that her natal Sun is in the 12th House, and as soon as I start asking, her answers give me numerous and spectacular confirmations. For example, she has a bunion on both feet.

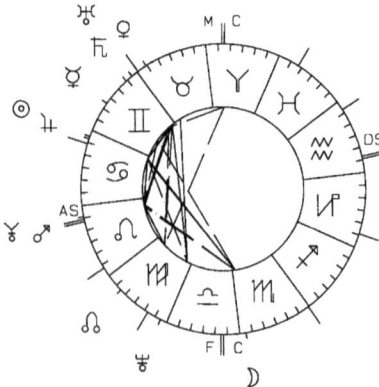

Birth chart, birth time 8:20 am

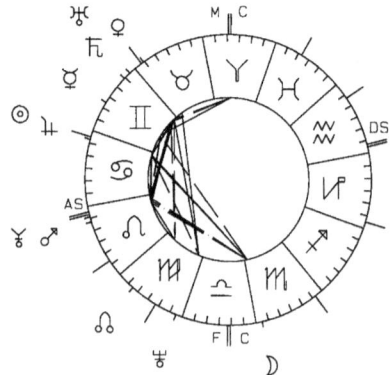

Birth chart, birth time 8:05 am

She suffered from several ingrown toenails, fractures and injuries to the foot. For long years she had been assisting both parents, spending many sleepless nights with them at the hospital, and even giving injections all the time.

She has health problems associated with both the heart and the stomach. She also has an exceptional mental and physical energy. For the time being, I provisionally consider the she may be born at 8:05.

7.
An essential astrological bibliography

- Various Authors: *Articles appeared on the quarterly* Ricerca '90 *from 1990 to 2008*, Edizioni Ricerca '90, 128 pp.

- Various Authors: *Special university issue (#45-46) of* l'astrologue, Éditions Traditionnelles, Paris

- John M. Addey: *Ritmi armonici in astrologia [Harmonic rhythms in astrology]*, Elefante ed., Catania, 1979, 352 pp.

- Antonino Anzaldi, Luigi Bazzoli: *Dizionario di Astrologia [Dictionary of astrology]*, BUR, Milan, 1988, 470 pp.

- Francesco Aulizio and Domenico Cafarello: *Considerazioni preliminari su un nuovo modo di studiare l'astrologia [Preliminary considerations about a new way of studying astrology]*, Cattedra di Storia della Medicina dell'Università di Bologna, Edizioni Capone, Turin

- André Barbault, H. Latou, B. Rossi, G. Simon: *Kepler*, Éditions Traditionnelles (l'astrologue *issue #52*), Paris

- André Barbault and Various Authors: *Soleil & Lune en Astrologie [Sun & Moon in Astrology]*, Publications du Centre International d'Astrologie, Paris, 1953, 280 pp.

- André Barbault: *Ariete [Aries]*, La Salamandra, Milan, 1985, 160 pp.

- André Barbault: *Astrologia e orientamento professionale [Astrology and professional orientation]*, Edizioni Ciro Discepolo, Naples, 1984, 93 pp.

- André Barbault: *Astrologia mondiale [World astrology]*, Armenia, Milan, 1980, 272 pp.

- André Barbault: *Dalla psicanalisi all'astrologia [From psychoanalysis to astrology]*, Morin, Siena, 1971, 224 pp.

- André Barbault: *Giove & Saturno [Jupiter & Saturn]*, Edizioni Ciro Discepolo, Naples, 1983, 214 pp.

- André Barbault: *Il pronostico sperimentale in astrologia [The experimental prediction in astrology]*, Mursia, Milan, 1979, 210 pp.

- André Barbault: *La Précession des Équinoxes et l'Astrologie [The precession of the equinoxes and Astrology]*, Centre International d'Astrologie, Paris, 1972, 32 pp.

- André Barbault, *La scienza dell'Astrologia [The science of Astrology]*, Nuovi Orizzonti, Milan, 1989, 186 pp.

- André Barbault: *L'astrologia e la previsione dell'avvenire [Astrology and the forecast of future]*, Armenia, Milan, 1993, 308 pp.

- André Barbault: *L'astrologia e l'avvenire del mondo [Astrology and the future of the world]*, Xenia, Milan, 1996, 212 pp.

- André Barbault: *Toro [Taurus]*, La Salamandra, Milan, 1985, 153 pp.

- André Barbault: *Trattato pratico di astrologia [A practical treatise of astrology]*, Morin, Siena, 1967, 317 pp.

- Armand Barbault: *Technique de l'interprétation [The technique of interpretation]*, Dervy Livres, Croissy-Beaubourg, 1991

- A. Barbault and others: *La luna nei miti e nello zodiaco [The Moon in the myths and in the Zodiac]*, Nuovi Orizzonti, Milan, 1989, 190 pp.

- Enzo Barillà and Ciro Discepolo: *Astrologia: sì e no [Astrology: yes and no]*, Edizioni Ricerca '90, Naples, 1994, 240 pp.

- Angelo Brunini: *L'avvenire non è un mistero [Future is not a mystery]*, published by the Author, Rome, 1964, 528 pp.

- Federico Capone: *Astronomia oroscopica [Horoscopic Astronomy]*, Edizioni Capone, Turin, 1977, 112 pp.

- Federico Capone: *Dizionario Astrologico [Astrological Dictionary]*, Edizioni Capone, Turin, 1978, 224 pp.

- Charles E.O. Carter: *An Introduction to Political Astrology*, Fowler, London, 1951, 104 pp.

- Charles E.O. Carter: *The Astrological Aspects*, Fowler, London, 1930, 160 pp.

- Charles E.O. Carter: *The Astrology of Accidents*, The Theosophical Publishing House Ltd., London, Unknown date of publishing, 124 pp.

- Charles E.O. Carter: *The Principles of Astrology*, The Theosophical Publishing House Ltd., London, 1925, 190 pp.

- Marco Celada: *Articles appeared on the quarterly* Ricerca '90 *from 1990 to 2008*, Edizione Ricerca '90, 128 pp.

- Yves Christiaen: *La Domification [Domification]*, Dervy Livres, Paris, 1978, 40 pp.

- Nicholas De Vore,: *Encyclopedia of Astrology*, Littlefield Adams and Co., New Jersey, U.S.A., 1977

- Arato Di Soli: *I fenomeni ed i pronostici [Phenomena and predictions]*, Arktos, Turin, 1984, 120 pp.

- Ciro Discepolo and Andrea Rossetti: *Astro & Geografia [Astro & Geography]*, Blue Diamond Publisher, Milan, 1996, 102 pp.

- Ciro Discepolo and Various Authors: *Osservazioni politematiche sulle ricerche Discepolo/Miele [Polithematic remarks on the researches of Discepolo & Miele]*, Edizioni Ricerca '90, Naples, 1992, 196 pp.

- Ciro Discepolo and Various Authors: *Per una rifondazione dell'astrologia o per il suo rifiuto [For a refoundation of Astrology or for its refusal]*, Edizioni Ricerca '90, Naples, 1993, 200 pp.

- Ciro Discepolo and Francesco Maggiore: *Elementi di astrology professionale [Elements of professional astrology]*, Blue Diamond Publisher, Milan, 1996, 93 pp.

- Ciro Discepolo and Francesco Maggiore: *Introduzione alla sinastria [An introduction to synastry]*, Blue Diamond Publisher, Milan, 1996, 106 pp.

- Ciro Discepolo and Luigi Galli: *Supporto tecnico alla pratica delle Rivoluzioni solari mirate [Technical support to the practise of Aimed Solar Returns]*, Blue Diamond Publisher, Milan, 2000, 136 pp.*

- Ciro Discepolo: *Astrologia applicata [Applied astrology]*, Armenia, Milan, 1988, 294 pp.

- Ciro Discepolo: *La ricerca dell'ora di nascita [The quest for the time of birth]*, Edizioni Ricerca '90, Naples, 1994, 64 pp.*

- Ciro Discepolo: *Astrologia Attiva [Active Astrology]*, Edizioni Mediterranee, Rome, 1998, 144 pp.*

- Ciro Discepolo: *Come scoprire i segreti di un oroscopo [How to unveil the secrets of a horoscope]*, Albero ed., Milan, 1988, 253 pp.

- Ciro Discepolo: *Esercizi sulle Rivoluzioni solari mirate [Exercises of Aimed Solar Returns]*, Blue Diamond Publisher, Milan, 1996, 96 pp.*

- Ciro Discepolo: *Guida ai transiti* (prima e seconda edizione) *[A guide to transits – 1st and 2nd edition]*, Armenia, Milan, 1984, 510 pp.*

- Ciro Discepolo: *Il sale dell'astrologia [The salt of astrology]*, Edizioni Capone, Turin, 1991, 144 pp.

- Ciro Discepolo: *Nuova guida all'astrologia [A new guide to astrology]*, Armenia, Milan, 2000, 818 pp.*

- Ciro Discepolo: *Nuovo dizionario di astrologia [The new Dictionary of Astrology]*, Armenia, Milan, 1996, 394 pp.*

- Ciro Discepolo: *Nuovo trattato delle Rivoluzioni solari [The new treatise of Solar Returns]*, Armenia, Milan, 2003, 216 pp.*

- Ciro Discepolo: *Piccola guida all'astrologia [A concise guide to astrology]*, Armenia, Milan, 1998, 200 pp.

- Ciro Discepolo: *Suite of software modules ASTRAL*, developed by the Author and Luigi Miele, Naples, 1979-2003

- Ciro Discepolo: *Prontuario calcoli [Ready reckoner]*, Edizioni Capone, Turin, 1979, 72 pp.

- Ciro Discepolo: *Quattro cose sui compleanni mirati [A few facts on Aimed Birthdays]*, Blue Diamond Publisher, Milan, 2001, 104 pp.*

- Ciro Discepolo: *Traité complet d'interprétation des transits et des Révolutions solaires en astrologie*, Éditions Traditionnelles, Paris, 2001, 502 pp.*

- Ciro Discepolo: *Transiti e Rivoluzioni solari [Transits and Solar Returns]*, Armenia, Milan, 1997, 502 pp.*

- Ciro Discepolo: *Trattato pratico di Rivoluzioni solari [A practical treatise of Solar Returns]*, Edizioni Ricerca '90, Naples, 1993, 208 pp.*

- Ciro Discepolo: *Various volumes of ephemerides*, Various publishers

- Ciro Discepolo: *Various volumes of Tables of Houses*, Various publishers

- Ciro Discepolo: *Ci siamo con la datazione informatica degli avvenimenti? [How far have we gone with the computerized dating of events?]*, Edizioni Ricerca '90, 2007, 168 pp.*

- Ciro Discepolo: *365 nap alatt a Föld körül a szolárhoroszkóppal*, DFT-Húngaria, Budapest, May 2006, 190 pp. B5*

- Ciro Discepolo: *Temelji medicinske astrologije: osnove za razumevanje clovekove patologije s pomocjo nebesnih teles,*

Zalozba Astroloskega instituta, 2007, pp. 262*

- Ciro Discepolo: *I fondamenti dell'Astrologia Medica [The fundaments of Medical Astrology]*, Armenia, Milan, end of January 2006, 246 pp.*

- Ciro Discepolo: *L'interpretazione del tema natale [Reading the natal chart]*, Armenia, Milan, September 2007, 336 pp.*

- Ciro Discepolo: *Transits and Solar Returns*, Naples, Ricerca '90 Publisher, September 2007, 560 pp.*

- Ciro Discepolo: Russian edition of the 'Nuovo Trattato delle Rivoluzioni solari', end of 2008*

- Ciro Discepolo: *Enquête sur l'hérédité astrale*, issue #67 of *l'astrologue*, Éditions Traditionnelles, Paris, 1984

- Ciro Discepolo: *Statistique sur 834 nominations ministérielles*, issue #67 of *l'astrologue*, Éditions Traditionnelles, Paris, 1986

- Ciro Discepolo: *Nouvelle recherche sur l'hérédité astrale*, issue #106 of *l'astrologue*, Éditions Traditionnelles, Paris, 1994

- Ciro Discepolo: *L'Hérédité astrale sur 50 000 naissances*, and *Astrologie activiste – Réflexions sur l'astrologie*, issue #125 of *l'astrologue*, Éditions Traditionnelles, Paris, 1999

- Reinhold Ebertin: *Cosmobiologia: la nuova astrologia [Cosmobiology: the new Astrology]*, Edizioni C.E.M., Naples, 1982, 208 pp.

- Michael Erlewine: *Manual of Computer Programming for Astrologers*, American Federation of Astrologers, Tempe (Arizona), 1980, 215 pp.

- Hans J. Eysenck, S. Mayo, O. White: *Un metodo empirico sul rapporto tra fattori astrologici e personalità [An empirical method on the relationship between astrological factors and peersonality]*, issue #42 of *Linguaggio astrale*, Turin, 1981

- Serena Foglia: *Prolusione al convegno di studi astrologici tenutosi a Napoli nel 1979 [Opening speech at the congress of astrological studies held in Naples in 1979]*, issue #37 of *Linguaggio Astrale*, Turin

- H. Freiherr Von Klöckler, *Corso di astrologia [Course on Astrology]*, ed. Mediterranee, Rome, 1979

- Luigi Galli and Ciro Discepolo: *Atlante geografico per le Rivoluzioni solari [Geographical Atlas for Solar Returns]*, Blue Diamond Publisher, Milan, 2001, 136 pp.*

- Luigi Galli: *Articles appeared on the quarterly* Ricerca '90 *from 1990 to 2008*, Edizioni Ricerca '90, Naples, 128 pp.

- Michel & Françoise Gauquelin: *Actors & politicians*, Laboratoire d'étude des relations entre rythmes cosmiques et psychophysiologiques, Paris, 1970

- Michel Gauquelin: *Il dossier delle influenze cosmiche [The file of cosmic influences]*, Astrolabio, Rome, 1975, 232 pp.

- Michel Gauquelin: *La Cosmopsychologie*, Retz, Paris, 1974, 256 pp.

- Michel Gauquelin: *L'astrologia di fronte alla scienza [Astrology face to science]*, Armenia, Milan, 1981, 312 pp.

- Michel & Françoise Gauquelin: *Méthodes pour étudier la répartition des astres dans le mouvement diurne,* Gauquelin ed., Paris, 1970

- Michel & Françoise Gauquelin: *Painters and musicians*, Laboratoire d'étude des relations entre rythmes cosmiques et psychophysiologiques, Paris, 1970

- Françoise Gauquelin: *Problèmes de l'heure risolus en astrologie*, Guy Trédaniel

- Michel Gauquelin: *Ritmi biologici e ritmi cosmici [Biological rhythms and cosmic rhythms]*, Faenza spa, Faenza, 1976, 226 pp.

- Luigi Gedda and Gianni Brenci: *Cronogenetica [Chronogenetics],* Est-Mondadori, Milan, 1974

- Sergio Ghivarello: *La realtà al di là dell'astrologia [Reality beyond astrology]*, Edizioni Capone, Turin

- Sergio Ghivarello: *L'astrologia e la teoria dei cicli nel quadro dei fenomeni ondulatori [Astrology and the theory of cycles withing the frame of undulatory phenomena]*, C.I.D.A. ed., Turin, 1974

- Sergio Ghivarello: *Lo zodiaco siderale e le costellazioni boreali [Sidereal Zodiac and Boreal constellations]*, #43/44/45, C.I.D.A. ed., Turin, 1981

- Sergio Ghivarello: *Verso una scienza alternativa [Towards an alternative science]*, issue #37 of *Linguaggio Astrale*, Turin, 1979

- Henri J. Gouchon and Jean Reverchon: *Dictionnaire Astrologique – Supplément Technique*, H. Gouchon Éditeur, Paris, 1947, 40 pp.

- Henri J. Gouchon: *Dizionario di astrologia [Dictionary of astrology]*, Siad ed., Milan, 1980

- Henri J. Gouchon: *Les Directions Primaires Simplifiées*, Éditions

Traditionnelles, Paris, 1970, ca. 150 pp.

- Henri J. Gouchon: *L'Horoscope Annuel Simplifié*, Dervy Livres, Paris, 1973, 214 pp.

- Hadès: *Guide pratique de l'interprétation en Astrologie*, Éditions Niclaus, Paris, 1969, 228 pp.

- Robert Hand: *I transiti [The transits]*, Armenia, Milan, 1982, 512 pp.

- Eugen Jonas: *Articles appeared on the quarterly* Ricerca '90 *from 1990 to 2008*, Edizioni Ricerca '90, Naples, 128 pp.

- Eugen Jonas: *Il controllo naturale del concepimento [The natural control of conception]*, Blue Diamond Publisher, Milan, 1995, 76 pp.

- Helene Kinauer Saltarini: *Bioritmo [Biorhythm]*, Siad ed., Milan, 1977

- George C. Noonan: *Spherical Astronomy for Astrologers*, American Federation of Astrologers, Washington DC, 1974, 62 pp.

- Tommaso Palamidessi: *Astrologia mondiale [World astrology]*, Archeosofica P., Rome, 1941, 588 pp.

- Johanna Paungger and Thomas Poppe: *La Luna ci insegna a star bene [The Moon teaches us how to be fine]*, Frasnelli - Keitsch, Bolzano/Bozen, 1995, 260 pp.

- Johanna Paungger and Thomas Poppe: *Servirsi della Luna [To use the Moon]*, Frasnelli - Keitsch, Bolzano/Bozen, 1995, 166 pp.

- Mariagrazia Pelaia: *Articles appeared on the quarterly* Ricerca '90 *from 1990 to 2008*, Edizione Ricerca '90, 128 pp.

- Andrea Rossetti: *Articles appeared on the quarterly* Ricerca '90 *from 1990 to 2008*, Edizioni Ricerca '90, Naples, 128 pp.

- Andrea Rossetti: *Breve trattato sui transiti [A concise treatise on transits]*, Blue Diamond Publisher, Milan, 1994, 125 pp.

- Andrea Rossetti: *Transiti, rivoluzioni solari e dasa indù [Transits, Solar Returns, and Hindu Dhasas]*, Blue Diamond Publisher, Milan, 1997, 188 pp.

- Alexander Ruperti: *I cicli del divenire [The cycles of becoming]*, Astrolabio, Rome, 1990, 301 pp.

- Frances Sakoian and Louis Acker: *Transits of Jupiter*, CSA Printing and Bindery Inc., USA, 1974, 72 pp.

- Frances Sakoian and Louis Acker: *Transits of Saturn*, CSA Printing and Bindery Inc., USA, 1973, 76 pp.

- Frances Sakoian and Louis Acker: *Transits of Uranus*, CSA Printing and Bindery Inc., USA, 1973, 78 pp.

- Vanda Sawtell: *Astrology & Biochemistry*, Rustington, Sussex, England, 86 pp.

- Françoise Secret: *Astrologie et alchimie au XVII siecle*, Studi francesi, new serie, vol. 60, issue #3

- Nicola Sementovsky-Kurilo: *Trattato completo di astrologia teorico e pratico [A complete theoretical-practical treatise of astrology]*, Hoepli ed., Milan, 1989

- Heber J. Smith: *Transits*, American Federation of Astrology, Tempe (Arizona), Unknown date of publishing, 42 pp.

- Kichinosuke Tatai: *I bioritmi [The biorhythms]*, ed. Mediterranee, Rome

- George S. Thommen: *Bioritmi [Biorhythms]*, Cesco Ciapanna ed.

- Claudius Ptolemy: *Descrizione della sfera celeste [Description of the Celestial Sphere]*, Arnaldo Forni, Bologna, 1990, 96 pp.

- Claudius Ptolemy: *Tetrabiblos, Le previsioni astrologiche [Tetrabiblos – the astrological predictions]*, Mondadori, Milan, 1985, 490 pp.

- Claudius Ptolemy: *Tetrabiblos*, Arktos, Carmagnola, 1980

- Claudius Ptolemy: *Tetrabiblos*, Arktos, Turin, 1979, 270 pp.

- Alexander Volguine: *Tecnica delle rivoluzioni solari [Technique of Solar Returs]*, Armenia, Milan, 1980, 226 pp.

- Herbert Von Klöckler, *Astrologia, scienza sperimentale [Astrology – an experimental science]*, Mediterranee, Rome, 1993, 183 pp.

- Ritchie R. Ward: *Gli orologi viventi [The living clocks]*, Bompiani, Milan, 1973

- Lyall Watson: *Supernatura [Supernature]*, Rizzoli ed, Milan, 1974

- David Williams: *Simplified Astronomy for Astrologers*, American Federation of Astrologers, Washington DC 1969, 90 pp.

* These are writings that deal – partly or extensively – with the subject 'Solar Returns' and 'Lunar Returns'.

Index

Preface .... pag.   7

1.   The rectification of the time of birth .... pag. 10

2.   The Sun in the twelve natal Houses .... pag. 16

3.   Positioning the 'sensors' .... pag. 50

4.   The entrance of Mars in the natal Houses .... pag. 55

5.   Transits of Mars .... pag. 57

6.   The interrogation .... pag. 73

7.   An essential astrological bibliography .... pag. 148

www.ingramcontent.com/pod-product-compliance
Lightning Source LLC
Chambersburg PA
CBHW050020100426
42739CB00011B/2724